Aldous Huxley

was born on 26 July 1894 near Godalming, Surrey. He began writing poetry and short stories in his early twenties, but it was his first novel, *Crome Yellow* (1921), which established his literary reputation. This was swiftly followed by *Antic Hay* (1923), *Those Barren Leaves* (1925) and *Point Counter Point* (1928) – bright, brilliant satires in which Huxley wittily but ruthlessly passed judgement on the shortcomings of contemporary society. For most of the 1920s Huxley lived in Italy and an account of his experiences there can be found in *Along the Road* (1925).

In the years leading up to the Second World War, Huxley's work took on a more sombre tone in response to the confusion of a society which he felt to be spinning dangerously out of control. The great novels of ideas, including his most famous work *Brave New World* (published in 1932 this warned against the dehumanising aspects of scientific and material 'progress') and the pacifist novel *Eyeless in Gaza* (1936) were accompanied by a series of wise and brilliant essays, collected in volume form under such titles as *Music at Night* (1931) and *Ends and Means* (1937).

In 1937, at the height of his fame, Huxley left Europe to live in California, working for a time as a screenwriter in Hollywood. As the West braced itself for war, Huxley came increasingly to believe that the key to solving the world's problems lay in changing the individual through mystical enlightenment. The exploration of the inner life through mysticism and hallucinogenic drugs was to dominate his work for the rest of his life. His beliefs found expression in both fiction (*Time Must Have A Stop*, 1944 and *Island*, 1962) and non-fiction (*The Perennial Philosophy*, 1945, *Grey Eminence*, 1941 and the famous account of his first mescalin experience, *The Doors of Perception*, 1954).

Huxley died in California on 22 November 1963.

MODERN CLASSIC

ALDOUS HUXLEY

Brave New World
Revisited

With an introduction by David Bradshaw

Flamingo

An Imprint of HarperCollins*Publishers*

Flamingo
An Imprint of HarperCollins*Publishers*
77–85 Fulham Palace Road,
Hammersmith, London W6 8JB

www.**fire**and**water**.com

A Flamingo Modern Classic 1994
9 8

Previously published in paperback by Grafton 1983
Reprinted five times

First published in Great Britain by
Chatto & Windus Ltd 1959

ISBN 0 00 654580 7

Set in Baskerville

Printed and bound in Great Britain by
Omnia Books Limited, Glasgow

CONTENTS

ALDOUS HUXLEY (1894–1963)

On 26 July 1894, near Godalming in Surrey, Aldous Leonard Huxley was born into a family which had only recently become synonymous with the intellectual aristocracy. Huxley's grandfather, Thomas Henry Huxley, had earned notoriety as 'Darwin's bulldog' and fame as a populariser of science, just as his own probing and controversial works were destined to outrage and exhilarate readers and non-readers alike in the following century. Aldous Huxley's mother was a niece of the poet and essayist Matthew Arnold, and he was a nephew of the redoubtable Mrs Humphry Ward, doyenne of late-Victorian novelists. This inheritance, combining the scientific and the literary in a blend which was to become characteristic of his vision as a writer, was both a source of great pride and a burden to Huxley in his formative years. Much was expected of him.

Three traumatic events left their mark on the young Huxley. In 1908 his mother died of cancer, and this led to the effective break-up of the family home. Two years later, while a schoolboy at Eton, Huxley contracted an eye infection which made him almost completely blind for a time and severely impaired his vision for the rest of his life. The suicide of his brother Trevenen in August 1914 robbed Huxley of the person to whom he felt closest. Over twenty years later, in *Eyeless in Gaza* (1936), Huxley's treatment of the death of the main character's mother and his embodiment of 'Trev' in the novel as the vulnerable Brian Foxe give some indication of the indelible pain which these tragic occurrences left in their wake. To a considerable degree, they account for the darkness, pungency and cynicism which feature so prominently in Huxley's work throughout the inter-war period.

Within months of achieving a First in English Language and

Literature at Balliol College, Oxford in 1916, Huxley published *The Burning Wheel*. Huxley's first collection of verse, and the three which followed it, *Jonah* (1917), *The Defeat of Youth* (1918) and *Leda* (1920), reveal his indebtedness to French symbolism and *fin de siècle* aestheticism. Also discernible, however, beneath the poetry's triste and ironic patina, is a concern with the inward world of the spirit which anticipates Huxley's later absorption in mysticism. These volumes of poetry were the first of over fifty separate works of fiction, drama, verse, criticism, biography, travel and speculative writing which Huxley was to produce during the course of his life.

Unfit for military service, Huxley worked as a farm labourer at Lady Ottoline Morrell's Garsington Manor after he left Oxford. Here he met not only D.H. Lawrence, Bertrand Russell, Clive Bell, Mark Gertler and other Bloomsbury figures, but also a Belgian refugee, Maria Nys, whom he married in 1919. By then Huxley was working for the *Athenaeum* magazine under the adroit editorship of Middleton Murry. Soon after he became the first British editor of *House and Garden*, worked for *Vogue* and contributed musical criticism to the *Weekly Westminster Gazette* in the early 1920s.

Limbo (1920), a collection of short stories, preceded the appearance of *Crome Yellow* in 1921, the novel with which Huxley first made his name as a writer. Inspired by, among others, Thomas Love Peacock, Norman Douglas and Anatole France, Huxley's first novel incorporated many incidents from his sojourn at Garsington as well as mischevious portraits of its chatelaine and his fellow guests. More blatantly still, *Crome Yellow* is an iconoclastic tilt at the Victorian and Edwardian mores which had resulted in the First World War and its terrible aftermath. For all its comic bravura, which won acclaim from writers such as Scott Fitzgerald and Max Beerbohm, *Crome Yellow* may be read, along with Lytton Strachey's *Eminent Victorians* (1918) and Huxley's second novel *Antic Hay* (1923), as an expression of the pervasive mood of disenchantment in the early 1920s. Huxley told his father that *Antic Hay* was 'written by a member of what I may call the war-generation for others of his kind'. He went on to say that it was intended to reflect 'the life and opinions of an age which has seen the violent disruption of almost all the standards, conventions and values current in the previous epoch'.

Even as a schoolboy Huxley had been an avid browser among the volumes of the *Encyclopaedia Britannica*, and it did not take long for him to acquire a reputation for arcane eclecticism. Moreover, as his prestige as a debunker and an emancipator grew, so Huxley was condemned more roundly by critics of the old guard, such as James Douglas of the *Daily Express*, who denounced the explicit discussion of sex and free thought in his fiction. *Antic Hay* was burned in Cairo, and in the ensuing years many of Huxley's books were censured, censored or banned at one time or another. Conversely, it was the openness, wit, effortless learning and apparent insouciance of Huxley's early work which proved such an appetising concoction for novelists as diverse as Evelyn Waugh, William Faulkner, Anthony Powell and Barbara Pym. Angus Wilson called Huxley 'the god of my adolescence'.

From 1923 onwards Huxley lived abroad more or less permanently, first near Florence and then, between 1930 and 1937, at Sanary on the Côte d'Azur. In *Along the Road* (1925), subtitled 'Notes and Essays of a Tourist', Huxley offered a lively and engaging account of the places and works of art he had taken in since his arrival in Italy, and both the title story of his third collection of tales, *Little Mexican* (1924), and his third novel, *Those Barren Leaves* (1925), are set in that country. According to Huxley, the theme of *Those Barren Leaves* is 'the undercutting of everything by a sort of despairing scepticism and then the undercutting of that by mysticism'. For W.B. Yeats, *Those Barren Leaves* heralded the return of philosophy to the English novel, but it was with his fourth novel, *Point Counter Point* (1928), that Huxley cemented his reputation with the reading public as a thought-provoking writer of fiction. *Point Counter Point* is Huxley's first true 'novel of ideas', the type of fiction with which he has become most closely identified. He once explained that his aim as a novelist was 'to arrive, technically, at a perfect fusion of the novel and the essay', arguing that the novel should be like a holdall, bursting with opinion and arresting ideas. This privileging of content over form was one of the many things he had in common with H.G. Wells; it was anathema to the likes of Virginia Woolf. Huxley was fascinated by the fact that 'the same person is simultaneously a mass of atoms, a physiology, a mind, an object with a shape that can be painted, a cog in the economic machine, a voter, a lover etc', and one of his key aims in *Point Counter Point* was to offer this multi-faceted view of his principal characters.

Huxley's more sombre mood in the late 1920s was epitomised by *Proper Studies* (1927), the most important of the four volumes of essays he published during the decade, and the one in which he first set himself unequivocally against what he regarded as the vulgarity and perversity of mass civilisation. Between September 1925 and June 1926 Huxley had travelled via India to the United States, and it was this visit to America which made him so pessimistic about the cultural future of Europe. He recounted his experiences in *Jesting Pilate* (1926). 'The thing which is happening in America is a revaluation of values,' Huxley wrote, 'a radical alteration (for the worse) of established standards', and it was soon after visiting the United States that Huxley conceived the idea of writing a satire on what he had encountered. *Brave New World* (1932) may be read as Huxley's contribution to the widespread fear of Americanisation which had been current in Europe since the mid-nineteenth century, but this humorous, disturbing and curiously ambivalent novel offers much more than straightforward travesty. Similarly, although *Brave New World* has become, with Orwell's *Nineteen Eighty-Four*, one of the twin pillars of the anti-utopian tradition in literature and a byword for all that is most repellent and 'nightmarish' in the world to come, it was written with Huxley's gaze very much on the crisis-torn present of Britain in 1931. When placed alongside *Brief Candles* (1930), a well-received collection of short stories, *Music at Night* (1931), a typically energetic and wide-ranging volume of essays, and *Texts and Pretexts* (1932), a verse anthology with commentaries designed to show that even in the highly-charged political atmosphere of the early 1930s 'they also serve who only bother their heads about art', Huxley's polygonal appeal as a novelist, thinker and pundit is brought home. In 1934 he published *Beyond the Mexique Bay*, an account of his travels in the Caribbean and Central America, and in 1936, *Eyeless in Gaza*. Stimulated by his conversion to pacifism in November 1935, Huxley's sixth novel imbricates the fears, foibles, prejudices and dissensions of the age with a fictionalisation of his own history. A commitment to questions which are essentially religious, rather than political or philosophical, is evident in Huxley's work for the first time.

When Huxley left Europe for the United States in April 1937 he was at the height of his fame as a novelist and the Peace Pledge Union's leading celebrity. Ironically, he was by now far more concerned with the virtues of non-attachment, anarchism, decentralisation and mystical salvation than with the failings of contemporary society, the role of pacifism in national politics or the art of fiction. If Huxley had been intent on exposing the meaninglessness of life in the 1920s, from the mid-1930s he was preoccupied with seeking the meaning of existence. *Ends and Means* (1937), in which Huxley tried 'to relate the problems of domestic and international politics, of war and economics, of education, religion and ethics, to a theory of the ultimate nature of reality', signalled his departure for the higher ground of mystical enlightenment where he would remain encamped for the rest of his life.

It was to lecture on the issues which dominate *Ends and Means* that Huxley and his friend and guru Gerald Heard had travelled to the United States. Huxley had every intention of returning to Europe, but his wife's need to live in a hot, dry climate on health grounds and the lucrative prospect of writing for the movies contrived to keep the Huxleys in America until it was too unsafe to return. Huxley's reaction to Hollywood and its cult of youth finds mordant expression in *After Many a Summer* (1939), the story of a Citizen Kane-like character's life of grandiose illusion. The materialist excesses of Jo Stoyte are counterpointed by the ascetic convictions of Propter, a modern-day anchorite modelled on Heard. Huxley and Hollywood were not compatible, and his failure to write a popular play in the inter-war years was mirrored in his largely unsuccessful efforts to write for the movies. Walt Disney's widely reported rejection of Huxley's synopsis of *Alice in Wonderland* on the grounds that he 'could only understand every third word' was symptomatic of Huxley's problem. His natural bent was for the leisurely and allusive development of an idea; above all else the movie moguls demanded pacey dialogue. His disenchantment with the world of the film studios is evident in the opening pages of *Ape and Essence* (1948), Huxley's ghastly and graphic projection of Los Angeles as a ruinous, sprawling ossuary in the aftermath of the atomic Third World War. While the threat of global nuclear conflict has receded for the present, Huxley's discussion of the rapid deforestation, pollution and other acts of ecological 'imbecility' which preceded the self-inflicted apocalypse he describes in the novel, is still chillingly topical.

Huxley spent most of the war years in a small house at Llano in the Mojave Desert in Southern California. In 1926 he had dismissed meditation as 'the doze's first cousin', but it was to a life of quietistic contemplation that Huxley now devoted himself. This phase of his career resulted in the excellent *Grey Eminence* (1941), a biography of Father Joseph, adviser to Cardinal Richelieu; *Time Must Have a Stop* (1944), a novel set in Florence in 1929 in which, to borrow Huxley's words, 'a piece of the *Comédie Humaine*. . . modulates into a version of the *Divina Commedia*'; and *The Perennial Philosophy* (1945), a profoundly influential anthology of excerpts and commentaries illustrating what Huxley called 'the highest common factor of all the higher religions'. He went on to say with typical humour and humility, 'The greatest merit of the book is that about forty per cent of it is not by me, but by a lot of saints, many of whom were also men of genius.' *The Devils of Loudun*, a compelling psychological study of sexual hysteria in seventeenth-century France, which was subsequently turned into a successful film, appeared in 1952. In the same way that Huxley's astringent social satires caught the mood of the 1920s, so, in the years during and following the Second World War and the enormity of the Jewish Holocaust, his personal concern with spiritual and ethical matters and his consternation at the accelerating arms race, reflected both the tone and unease of the zeitgeist.

Huxley also acquired new readers through his support of the marginal and unconventional, and his detractors, hitherto exercised by what they saw as his immorality or preachiness, began to pour scorn on his alleged faddism. In 1942 he published *The Art of Seeing*, a passionate defence of the Bates method of eye training which aroused a storm of protest from the optometrist lobby. Even more outrageous, for many, was his suggestion in *The Doors of Perception* (1954) and its sequel, *Heaven and Hell* (1956), that mescalin and lysergic acid were 'drugs of unique distinction' which should be exploited for the 'supernaturally brilliant' visionary experiences they offered to those with open minds and sound livers. *The Doors of Perception* is indeed a bewitching account of the inner shangri-la of the mescalin taker, where 'there is neither work nor monotony' but only 'a perpetual present made up of one continually changing apocalypse', where 'the divine source of all existence' is evident in a vase of flowers, and even the creases in a pair of trousers reveal 'a labyrinth of endlessly significant complexity'. Not surprisingly, *The Doors of Perception* became a set text for the beat generation and the psychedelic Sixties, The Doors naming their band after the book which also earned Huxley a place on the sleeve of The Beatles' *Sergeant Pepper* album.

Maria Huxley died in February 1955, shortly before Huxley published his penultimate novel, *The Genius and the Goddess*, in which John Rivers recounts the brief history of his disastrous involvement, when he was a 'virgin prig of twenty-eight', with the wife of his colleague Henry Maartens, a Nobel Prize-winning scientist. Not for the first time, Huxley's theme is the havoc which ensues when a man with an idealistic misconception of life born of a cloistered and emotionally deprived upbringing experiences the full, sensual impact of human passion.

Huxley married Laura Archera, a practising psychotherapist, in March 1956. Two years later he published *Brave New World Revisited*, in which he surveyed contemporary society in the light of his earlier predictions. Huxley's knack of keying in to the anxieties of the moment was as sharp as ever, and this touch is also evident in a series of lectures on 'The Human Situation' which he gave at Santa Barbara in 1959, published in one volume in 1977. Both books address problems which are no less pressing today, such as overpopulation, the recrudescence of nationalism and the fragility of the natural world. Huxley's last novel, *Island*, was published in 1962, the year in which he was made a Companion of Literature, and the year after his Los Angeles home and most of his personal effects had been destroyed in a fire which, Huxley said, left him 'a man without possessions and without a past'.

Island is the story of how the offshore utopia of Pala, where population growth has been stabilised and Mutual Adoption Clubs have superseded the tyranny of the family, and where *maithuna*, or the yoga of love and *moksha*, an hallucinogenic toadstool, ensure that the Palanese have little reason to feel disgruntled, falls victim to the age-old menaces of material progress and territorial expansionism. *Island* is perhaps Huxley's most pessimistic book, his poignant acknowledgement that in a world of increasing greed, mass communication, oil-guzzling transport, burgeoning population and inveterate hostility, a pacific and co-operative community like Pala's 'oasis of freedom and happiness' has little hope of survival. Soon after *Island* was published Huxley commented that the 'weakness of the book consists in a disbalance between fable and exposition. The story has too much weight, in the way of ideas and reflections, to carry.' But, while some readers would agree with this criticism, for others *Island* exemplifies Huxley's particular contribution to twentieth-century letters. In his early days the highbrow incarnate and a reluctant lecturer for the Peace Pledge Union, Huxley became for many a companionable polymath, a transatlantic sage at large, whose unending quest for synthesis and meaning in an ever-more perplexing and violent world provided a paradigm for their own search for peace and understanding.

Before his eyesight was damaged, Huxley's ambition was to specialise in the sciences, and it is significant that in his last published work, *Literature and Science* (1963), he pleads yet again for a *rapprochement* between the two cultures, arguing passionately against the contemporary stress on their dichotomy. The book begins by emphasising the wide-ranging erudition of T.H. Huxley and Matthew Arnold. Their descendant, one of the most stimulating and provocative writers of the twentieth century, proved himself a worthy inheritor of their abilities over the course of his long and varied career.

Huxley died of cancer at his home in Hollywood on 22 November 1963, unaware that President J.F. Kennedy had been assassinated earlier that afternoon in Dallas. In 1971 his ashes were returned to England and interred in his parents' grave at Compton in Surrey.

David Bradshaw
Worcester College, Oxford
1993

Foreword

The soul of wit may become the very body of
untruth. However elegant and memorable, brevity
can never, in the nature of things, do justice to all
the facts of a complex situation. On such a theme
one can be brief only by omission and simplification. Omission and simplification help us to
understand – but help us, in many cases, to understand the wrong thing; for our comprehension may
be only of the abbreviator's neatly formulated
notions, not of the vast, ramifying reality from
which these notions have been so arbitrarily
abstracted.

But life is short and information endless: nobody
has time for everything. In practice we are
generally forced to choose between an unduly brief
exposition and no exposition at all. Abbreviation is
a necessary evil and the abbreviator's business is to
make the best of a job which, though intrinsically
bad, is still better than nothing. He must learn to
simplify, but not to the point of falsification. He
must learn to concentrate upon the essentials of a
situation, but without ignoring too many of reality's qualifying side-issues. In this way he may be
able to tell not indeed the whole truth (for the

whole truth about almost any important subject is incompatible with brevity), but considerably more than the dangerous quarter-truths and half-truths which have always been the current coin of thought.

The subject of freedom and its enemies is enormous, and what I have written is certainly too short to do it full justice; but at least I have touched on many aspects of the problem. Each aspect may have been somewhat over-simplified in the exposition; but these successive over-simplifications add up to a picture that, I hope, gives some hint of the vastness and complexity of the original.

Omitted from the picture (not as being unimportant, but merely for convenience and because I have discussed them on earlier occasions) are the mechanical and military enemies of freedom – the weapons and gadgets which have so powerfully strengthened the hands of the world's rulers against their subjects, and the ever more ruinously costly preparations for ever more senseless and suicidal wars. The chapters that follow should be read against a background of thoughts about the Hungarian uprising and its repression, about the H-bombs, about the cost of what every nation refers to as 'defence', about those endless columns of uniformed boys, white, black, brown, yellow, marching obediently towards the common grave.

I

Overpopulation

In 1931, when *Brave New World* was being written, I was convinced that there was still plenty of time. The completely organized society, the scientific caste system, the abolition of free will by methodical conditioning, the servitude made acceptable by regular doses of chemically induced happiness, the orthodoxies drummed in by nightly courses of sleep-teaching – these things were coming all right, but not in my time, not even in the time of my grandchildren. I forget the exact date of the events recorded in *Brave New World*; but it was somewhere in the sixth or seventh century A.F. (after Ford). We who were living in the second quarter of the twentieth century A.D. were the inhabitants, admittedly, of a gruesome kind of universe; but the nightmare of those depression years was radically different from the nightmare of the future, described in *Brave New World*. Ours was a nightmare of too little order; theirs, in the seventh century A.F., of too much. In the process of passing from one extreme to the other, there would be a long interval, so I imagined, during which the more fortunate third of the human race would make the best of both worlds – the disorderly world of liberalism and the much too orderly Brave New World where perfect efficiency left no room for freedom or personal initiative.

Twenty-seven years later, in this third quarter of the twentieth century A.D., and long before the end of the first century A.F., I feel a good deal less optimistic than I did when I was writing *Brave New World*. The prophecies made in 1931 are coming true much sooner than I thought they would. The blessed interval between too little order and the nightmare of too much has not begun and shows no sign of beginning. In the West, it is true, individual men and women still enjoy a large measure of freedom. But even in those countries that have a tradition of democratic government, this freedom and even the desire for this freedom seems to be on the wane. In the rest of the world freedom for individuals has already gone, or is manifestly about to go. The nightmare of total organization, which I had situated in the seventh century after Ford, has emerged from the safe, remote future and is now awaiting us, just around the next corner.

George Orwell's *1984* was a magnified projection into the future of a present that contained Stalinism and an immediate past that had witnessed the flowering of Nazism. *Brave New World* was written before the rise of Hitler to supreme power in Germany and when the Russian tyrant had not yet got into his stride. In 1931 systematic terrorism was not the obsessive contemporary fact which it had become in 1948, and the future dictatorship of my imaginary world was a good deal less brutal than the future dictatorship so brilliantly portrayed by Orwell. In the context of 1948, *1984* seemed dreadfully convincing. But tyrants, after all, are mortal and circumstances change. Recent developments in Russia, and recent advances in science and technology, have robbed Orwell's book of some of its gruesome verisimilitude. A nuclear war will, of course, make nonsense of everybody's predictions. But, assuming for the moment that the Great Powers can somehow refrain from destroying us, we can say that it now looks as though the odds were more in favour of something like *Brave New World* than of something like *1984*.

In the light of what we have recently learned about animal behaviour in general, and human behaviour in particular, it has become clear that control through the punishment of undesirable behaviour is less effective, in the long run, than control through the reinforcement of desirable behaviour by rewards, and that government through terror works on the whole less well than government through the non-violent manipulation of the environment and of the thoughts and feelings of the individual men, women and children. Punishment temporarily puts a stop to undesirable behaviour, but does not permanently reduce the victim's tendency to indulge in it. Moreover, the psycho-physical by-products of punishment may be just as undesirable as the behaviour for which an individual has been punished. Psycho-therapy is largely concerned with the debilitating or anti-social consequences of past punishments.

The society described in *1984* is a society controlled almost exclusively by punishment and the fear of punishment. In the imaginary world of my own fables, punishment is infrequent and generally mild. The nearly perfect control exercised by the government is achieved by systematic reinforcement of desirable behaviour, by many kinds of nearly non-violent manipulation, both physical and psychological, and by genetic standardization. Babies in bottles and the centralized control of reproduction are not perhaps impossible; but it is quite clear that for a long time to come we shall remain a viviparous species breeding at random. For practical purposes genetic standardization may be ruled out. Societies will continue to be controlled post-natally – by punishment, as in the past, and to an ever-increasing extent by the more effective methods of reward and scientific manipulation.

In Russia the old-fashioned, *1984*-style dictatorship of Stalin has begun to give way to a more up-to-date form of tyranny. In the upper levels of the Soviets' hierarchical society the reinforcement of desirable behaviour has begun to replace the older methods of control through the punishment of undesirable behaviour. Engineers and scientists, teachers and administrators, are handsomely paid for good work and so moderately taxed that they are under constant incentive to do better and so be more highly rewarded. In certain areas they are at liberty to think and do more or less what they like. Punishment awaits them only when they stray beyond their prescribed limits into the realms of ideology and politics. It is because they have been granted a measure of professional freedom that Russian teachers, scientists and technicians have achieved such remarkable successes. Those who live near the base of the Soviet pyramid enjoy none of the privileges accorded to the lucky or specially gifted minority. Their wages are meagre and they pay, in the form of high prices, a disproportionately large share of the taxes. The area in which they can do as they please is extremely restricted, and their rulers control them more by punishment and the threat of punishment than through non-violent manipulation or the reinforcement of desirable behaviour by reward. The Soviet system combines elements of *1984* with elements that are prophetic of what went on among the higher castes in *Brave New World*.

Meanwhile impersonal forces over which we have almost no control seem to be pushing us all in the direction of the Brave New Worldian nightmare; and this impersonal pushing is being consciously accelerated by representatives of commercial and political organizations who have developed a number of new techniques for manipulating, in the interests of some minority, the thoughts and feelings of the masses. The techniques of manipulation will be discussed in later chapters. For the moment let us confine our attentions to those impersonal forces which are now making the world so extremely unsafe for democracy, so very inhospitable to individual freedom. What are these forces? And why has the nightmare which I had projected into the seventh century A.F., made so swift an advance in our direction? The answer to these questions must begin where the life of even the most highly civilized society has its beginnings – on the level of biology.

On the first Christmas Day the population of our planet was about two hundred and fifty millions – less than half the population of modern China. Sixteen centuries later, when the Pilgrim Fathers landed at Plymouth Rock, human numbers had climbed to a little more than five hundred millions. By the time of the signing of the Declaration of Independence, world population had passed the seven hundred million mark. In 1931, when I was writing *Brave New World*, it stood at just under

two billions. Today, only twenty-seven years
later, there are two thousand eight hundred million of us. And tomorrow – what? Penicillin,
DDT and clean water are cheap commodities,
whose effects on public health are out of all
proportion to their cost. Even the poorest government is rich enough to provide its subjects with a
substantial measure of death control. Birth control is a very different matter. Death control is
something which can be provided for a whole
people by a few technicians working in the pay of
a benevolent government. Birth control depends
on the co-operation of an entire people. It must be
practised by countless individuals, from whom it
demands more intelligence and will power than
most of the world's teeming illiterates possess,
and (where chemical or mechanical methods of
contraception are used) an expenditure of more
money than most of these millions can now afford.
Moreover, there are nowhere any religious traditions in favour of unrestricted death, whereas
religious and social traditions in favour of unrestricted reproduction are widespread. For all
these reasons, death control is achieved very
easily, birth control is achieved with great dif-
ficulty. Death rates have therefore fallen in recent
years with startling suddenness. But birth rates
have either remained at their old high level or, if
they have fallen, have fallen very little and at a
very slow rate. In consequence, human numbers

are now increasing more rapidly than at any time in the history of the species.

Moreover, the yearly increases are themselves increasing. They increase regularly, according to the rules of compound interest; and they also increase irregularly with every application, by a technologically backward society, of the principles of Public Health. At the present time the annual increase in the world population runs to about forty-three millions. This means that every four years mankind adds to its numbers the equivalent of the present population of the United States, every eight and a half years the equivalent of the present population of India. At the rate of increase prevailing between the birth of Christ and the death of Queen Elizabeth 1 it took sixteen centuries for the population of the earth to double. At the present rate it will double in less than half a century. And this fantastically rapid doubling of our numbers will be taking place on a planet whose most desirable and productive areas are already densely populated, whose soils are being eroded by the frantic efforts of bad farmers to raise more food, and whose easily available mineral capital is being squandered with the reckless extravagance of a drunken sailor getting rid of his accumulated pay.

In the Brave New World of my fable, the problem of human numbers in their relation to natural resources had been effectively solved. An optimum figure for world population had been calculated and numbers were maintained at this figure (a little under two billions, if I remember rightly) generation after generation. In the real contemporary world, the population problem has not been solved. On the contrary it is becoming graver and more formidable with every passing year. It is against this grim biological background that all the political, economic, cultural and psychological dramas of our time are being played out. As the twentieth century wears on, as the new billions are added to the existing billions (there will be more than five and a half billions of us by the time my granddaughter is fifty), this biological background will advance, ever more insistently, ever more menacingly, towards the front and centre of the historical stage. The problem of rapidly increasing numbers in relation to natural resources, to social stability and to the well being of individuals – this is now the central problem of mankind; and it will remain the central problem certainly for another century, and perhaps for several centuries thereafter. A new age is supposed to have begun on October 4th, 1957. But actually, in the present context, all our exuberant post-Sputnik talk is irrelevant and even nonsensical. So far as the masses of mankind are concerned, the coming time will not be the Space Age; it will be the Age of Overpopulation. We can parody the words of the old song and ask,

Will the space that you're so rich in
Light a fire in the kitchen,
Or the little god of space turn the spit, spit, spit?

The answer, it is obvious, is in the negative. A
settlement on the moon may be of some military
advantage to the nation that does the settling. But
it will do nothing whatever to make life more
tolerable, during the fifty years that it will take
our present population to double, for the earth's
undernourished and proliferating billions. And
even if, at some future date, emigration to Mars
should become feasible, even if any considerable
number of men and women were desperate
enough to choose a new life under conditions
comparable to those prevailing on a mountain
twice as high as Mount Everest, what difference
would that make? In the course of the last four
centuries quite a number of people sailed from the
Old World to the New. But neither their departure nor the returning flow of food and raw
materials could solve the problems of the Old
World. Similarly the shipping of a few surplus
humans to Mars (at a cost, for transportation and
development, of several million dollars a head)
will do nothing to solve the problem of mounting
population pressures on our own planet. Unsol-
ved, that problem will render insoluble all our
other problems. Worse still, it will create conditions in which individual freedom and the social

decencies of the democratic way of life will become impossible, almost unthinkable.

Not all dictatorships arise the same way. There are many roads to Brave New World; but perhaps the straightest and the broadest of them is the road we are travelling today, the road that leads through gigantic numbers and accelerating increases. Let us briefly review the reasons for this close correlation between too many people, too rapidly multiplying, and the formulation of authoritarian philosophies, the rise of totalitarian systems of government.

As large and increasing numbers press more heavily upon available resources, the economic position of the society undergoing this ordeal becomes ever more precarious. This is especially true of those underdeveloped regions, where a sudden lowering of the death rate by means of DDT, penicillin and clean water has not been accompanied by a corresponding fall in the birth rate. In parts of Asia and in most of Central and South America populations are increasing so fast that they will double themselves in little more than twenty years. If the production of food and manufactured articles, of houses, schools and teachers, could be increased at a greater rate than human numbers, it would be possible to improve the wretched lot of those who live in these underdeveloped and overpopulated countries. But unfortunately these countries lack not merely agricultural machinery and an industrial plant capable of turning out this machinery, but also the capital required to create such a plant. Capital is what is left over after the primary needs of a population have been satisfied. But the primary needs of most of the people in underdeveloped countries are never fully satisfied. At the end of each year almost nothing is left over, and there is almost no capital available for creating the industrial and agricultural plants, by means of which the people's needs might be satisfied. Moreover, there is, in all these underdeveloped countries, a serious shortage of the trained manpower without which a modern industrial and agricultural plant cannot be operated. The present educational facilities are inadequate; so are the resources, financial and cultural, for improving the existing facilities as fast as the situation demands. Meanwhile the population of some of these underdeveloped countries is increasing at the rate of three per cent per annum.

Their tragic situation is discussed in an important book, published in 1957 – *The Next Hundred Years*, by Professors Harrison Brown, James Bonner and John Weir of the California Institute of Technology. How is mankind coping with the problem of rapidly increasing numbers? Not very successfully. 'The evidence suggests rather strongly that in most underdeveloped countries the lot of the average individual has worsened appreciably in the last half-century. People have become more poorly fed. There are fewer available goods per person. And practically every attempt to improve the situation has been nullified by the relentless pressure of continued population growth.'

Whenever the economic life of a nation becomes precarious, the central government is forced to assume additional responsibilities for the general welfare. It must work out elaborate plans for dealing with a critical situation; it must impose ever greater restrictions upon the activities of its subjects; and if, as is very likely, worsening economic conditions result in political unrest, or open rebellion, the central government must intervene to preserve public order and its own authority. More and more power is thus concentrated in the hands of the executives and their bureaucratic managers. But the nature of power is such that even those who have not sought it, but have had it forced upon them, tend to acquire a taste for more. 'Lead us not into temptation,' we pray – and with good reason; for when human beings are tempted too enticingly or too long, they generally yield. A democratic constitution is a device for preventing the local rulers from yielding to those particularly dangerous temptations that arise when too much power is concentrated in too few hands. Such a constitution works pretty well where, as in Britain or the United States, there is a traditional respect for constitutional procedures. Where the republican or limited monarchical tradition is weak, the best of constitutions will not prevent ambitious politicians from succumbing with glee and gusto to the temptations of power. And in any country where numbers have begun to press heavily upon available resources, these temptations cannot fail to arise. Overpopulation leads to economic insecurity and social unrest. Unrest and insecurity lead to more control by central governments and an increase of their power. In the absence of a constitutional tradition, this increased power will probably be exercised in a dictatorial fashion. Even if Communism had never been invented, this would be likely to happen. But Communism has been invented. Given this fact, the probability of overpopulation leading through unrest to dictatorship becomes a virtual certainty. It is a pretty safe bet that, twenty years from now, all the world's overpopulated and underdeveloped countries will be under some form of totalitarian rule – probably by the Communist Party.

How will this development affect the overpopulated, but highly industrialized and still democratic countries of Europe? If the newly formed dictatorships were hostile to them, and if the normal flow of raw materials from the underdeveloped countries were deliberately interrupted, the nations of the West would find themselves in a very bad way indeed. Their industrial system would break down, and the highly developed technology, which up till now has permitted them to sustain a population much greater than that which could be supported by locally available resources, would no longer protect them against the consequences of having too many people in too small a territory. If this should happen, the enormous powers forced by unfavourable conditions upon central governments may come to be used in the spirit of totalitarian dictatorship.

The United States is not at present an overpopulated country. If, however, the population continues to increase at the present rate (which is higher than that of India's increase, though happily a good deal lower than the rate now current in Mexico or Guatemala), the problem of numbers in relation to available resources might well become troublesome by the beginning of the twenty-first century. For the moment overpopulation is not a direct threat to the personal freedom of Americans. It remains, however, an indirect threat, a menace at one remove. If overpopulation should drive the underdeveloped countries into totalitarianism, and if these new dictatorships should ally themselves with Russia, then the military position of the United States would become less secure and the preparations for defence and retaliation would have to be intensified. But liberty, as we all know, cannot flourish in a country that is permanently on a war footing, or even a near-war footing. Permanent crisis justifies permanent control of everybody and everything by the agencies of the central government. And permanent crisis is what we have to expect in a world in which overpopulation is producing a state of things in which dictatorship under Communist auspices becomes almost inevitable.

II

Quantity, Quality, Morality

In the Brave New World of my phantasy, euge-
nics and dysgenics were practised systematically.
In one set of bottles biologically superior ova,
fertilized by biologically superior sperm, were
given the best possible pre-natal treatment and
were finally decanted as Betas, Alphas and even
Alpha Pluses. In another, much more numerous
set of bottles, biologically inferior ova, fertilized
by biologically inferior sperm, were subjected to
the Bokanovsky Process (ninety-six identical
twins out of a single egg) and treated pre-natally
with alcohol and other protein poisons. The creatures finally decanted were almost sub-human;
but they were capable of performing unskilled
work and, when properly conditioned, deten-
sioned by free and frequent access to the opposite
sex, constantly distracted by gratuitous entertainment and reinforced in their good behaviour
patterns by daily doses of *soma*, could be counted
on to give no trouble to their superiors.

In this second half of the twentieth century we
do nothing systematic about our breeding; but in
our random and unregulated way we are not only
overpopulating our planet, we are also, it would

seem, making sure that these greater numbers shall be of biologically poorer quality. In the bad old days children with considerable, or even slight, hereditary defects rarely survived. Today, thanks to sanitation, modern pharmacology and the social conscience, most of the children born with hereditary defects reach maturity and multiply their kind. Under the conditions now prevailing, every advance in medicine will tend to be offset by a corresponding advance in the survival rates of individuals cursed by some genetic insufficiency. In spite of new wonder drugs and better treatment (indeed, in a certain sense, precisely because of these things), the physical health of the general population will show no improvement, and may even deteriorate. And along with a decline in average healthiness there may well go a decline in average intelligence. Indeed, some competent authorities are convinced that such a decline has already taken place and is continuing. 'Under conditions that are both soft and unregulated,' writes Dr W.H. Sheldon, 'our best stock tends to be outbred by stock that is inferior to it in every respect ... It is the fashion in some academic circles to assure students that the alarm over differential birth-rates is unfounded; that these problems are merely economic, or merely educational, or merely religious, or merely cultural or something of the sort. This is Pollyanna optimism. Reproductive delinquency is biological and basic.' And he adds that 'nobody knows just how far the average IQ in this country (the USA) has declined since 1916, when Terman attempted to standardize the meaning of IQ 100'.

In an underdeveloped and overpopulated country, where four-fifths of the people get less than 2000 calories a day and one-fifth enjoys an adequate diet, can democratic institutions arise spontaneously? Or if they should be imposed from outside or from above, can they possibly survive?

And now let us consider the case of the rich, industrialized and democratic society, in which, owing to the random but effective practice of dysgenics, IQ's and physical vigour are on the decline. For how long can such a society maintain its traditions of individual liberty and democratic government? Fifty or a hundred years from now our children will learn the answer to this question.

Meanwhile we find ourselves confronted by a most disturbing moral problem. We know that the pursuit of good ends does not justify the employment of bad means. But what about those situations, now of such frequent occurrence, in which good means have end results which turn out to be bad?

For example, we go to a tropical island and with the aid of DDT we stamp out malaria and, in two or three years, save hundreds of thousands of lives. This is obviously good. But the hundreds of thousands of human beings thus saved, and the millions whom they beget and bring to birth, cannot be adequately clothed, housed, educated or even fed out of the island's available resources. Quick death by malaria has been abolished; but life made miserable by undernourishment and overcrowding is now the rule and slow death by outright starvation threatens ever greater numbers.

And what about the congenitally insufficient organisms, whom our medicine and our social services now preserve so that they may propagate their kind? To help the unfortunate is obviously good. But the wholesale transmission to our descendants of the results of unfavourable mutations, and the progressive contamination of the genetic pool from which the members of our species will have to draw, are no less obviously bad. We are on the horns of an ethical dilemma, and to find the middle way will require all our intelligence and all our good will.

III

Over-organization

The shortest and broadest road to the nightmare of Brave New World leads, as I have pointed out, through overpopulation and the accelerating increase of human numbers – twenty-eight hundred millions today, fifty-five hundred millions by the turn of the century, with most of humanity facing the choice between anarchy and totalitarian control. But the increasing pressure of numbers upon available resources is not the only force propelling us in the direction of totalitarianism. This blind biological enemy of freedom is allied with immensely powerful forces generated by the very advances in technology of which we are most proud. Justifiably proud, it may be added; for these advances are the fruits of genius and persistent hard work, of logic, imagination and self-denial – in a word, of moral and intellectual virtues for which one can feel nothing but admiration. But the Nature of Things is such that nobody in this world ever gets anything for nothing. These amazing and admirable advances have to be paid for. Indeed, like last year's washing machine, they are still being paid for – and each instalment is higher than the last. Many historians, many sociologists and psychologists have written at length, and with deep concern, about the price that Western man has had to pay and will go on paying for technological progress. They point out, for example, that democracy can hardly be expected to flourish in societies where political and economic power is being progressively concentrated and centralized. But the progress of technology has led and is still leading to just such concentration and centralization of power. As the machinery of mass production is made more efficient it tends to become more complex and more expensive – and so less available to the enterpriser of limited means. Moreover, mass production cannot work without mass distribution; but mass distribution raises problems which only the largest producers can satisfactorily solve. In a world of mass production and mass distribution the Little Man, with his inadequate stock of working capital, is at a grave disadvantage. In competition with the Big Man, he loses his money and finally his very existence as an independent producer; the Big Man has gobbled him up. As the Little Men disappear, more and more economic power comes to be wielded by fewer and fewer people. Under a dictatorship the Big Business, made possible by advancing technology and the consequent ruin of Little Business, is controlled by the State – that is to say, by a small group of party leaders and the soldiers, policemen and civil servants who carry out their orders. In a capitalist democracy, such as the United States, it is controlled by what Professor C. Wright Mills has called the Power Elite. This Power Elite directly employs several millions of the country's working force in its factories, offices and stores, controls many millions more by lending them the money to buy its products, and, through its ownership of the media of mass communication, influences the thoughts, the feelings and the actions of virtually everybody. To parody the words of Winston Churchill, never have so many been manipulated so much by so few. We are far indeed from Jefferson's ideal of a genuinely free society composed of a hierarchy of self-governing units – 'the elementary republics of the wards, the county republics, the State republics and the Republic of the Union, forming a gradation of authorities.'

We see, then, that modern technology has led to the concentration of economic and political power, and to the development of a society controlled (ruthlessly in the totalitarian states, politely and inconspicuously in the democracies) by Big Business and Big Government. But societies are composed of individuals and are good only in so far as they help individuals to realize their potentialities and to lead a happy and fruitful life. How have individuals been affected by the technological advances of recent years? Here is the answer to this question given by a philosopher-psychiatrist, Dr Erich Fromm:

'Our contemporary Western society, in spite of its material, intellectual and political progress, is increasingly less conducive to mental health, and tends to undermine the inner security, happiness, reason and the capacity for love in the individual; it tends to turn him into an automaton who pays for his human failure with increasing mental sickness, and with despair hidden under a frantic drive for work and so-called pleasure.'

Our 'increasing mental sickness' may find expression in neurotic symptoms. These symptoms are conspicuous and extremely distressing. But 'let us beware', says Dr Fromm, 'of defining mental hygiene as the prevention of symptoms. Symptoms as such are not our enemy, but our friend; where there are symptoms there is conflict, and conflict always indicates that the forces of life which strive for integration and happiness are still fighting.' The really hopeless victims of mental illness are to be found among those who appear to be most normal. 'Many of them are normal because they are so well adjusted to our mode of existence, because their human voice has been silenced so early in their lives, that they do not even struggle or suffer or develop symptoms as the neurotic does.' They are normal not in what may be called the absolute sense of the word; they are normal only in relation to a profoundly abnor mal society. Their perfect adjustment to that abnormal society is a measure of their mental sickness. These millions of abnormally normal people, living without fuss in a society to which, if they were fully human beings, they ought not to be adjusted, still cherish 'the illusion of individuality', but in fact they have been to a great extent de-individualized. Their conformity is developing into something like uniformity. But 'uniformity and freedom are incompatible. Uniformity and mental health are incompatible too . . . Man is not made to be an automaton, and if he becomes one, the basis for mental health is destroyed.'

In the course of evolution nature has gone to endless trouble to see that every individual is unlike every other individual. We reproduce our kind by bringing the father's genes into contact with the mother's. These hereditary factors may be combined in an almost infinite number of ways. Physically and mentally, each one of us is unique. Any culture which, in the interests of efficiency or in the name of some political or religious dogma, seeks to standardize the human individual, commits an outrage against man's biological nature.

Science may be defined as the reduction of multiplicity to unity. It seeks to explain the endlessly diverse phenomena of nature by ignoring the uniqueness of particular events, concentrating on what they have in common and finally abstracting some kind of 'law', in terms of which they make sense and can be effectively dealt with. As examples, apples fall from the tree and the moon moves across the sky. People had been observing these facts from time immemorial. With Gertrude Stein they were convinced that an apple is an apple is an apple, whereas the moon is the moon is the moon. It remained for Isaac Newton to perceive what these very dissimilar phenomena had in common, and to formulate a theory of gravitation in terms of which certain aspects of the behaviour of apples, of the heavenly bodies and indeed of everything else in the physical universe could be explained and dealt with in terms of a single system of ideas. In the same spirit the artist takes the innumerable diversities and uniquenesses of the outer world and his own imagination and gives them meaning within an orderly system of plastic, literary or musical patterns. The wish to impose order upon confusion, to bring harmony out of dissonance and unity out of multiplicity, is a kind of intellectual instinct, a primary and fundamental urge of the mind. Within the realms of science, art and philosophy the workings of what I may call this 'Will to Order' are mainly beneficent. True, the Will to Order has produced many premature syntheses based upon insufficient evidence, many absurd systems of metaphysics and theology, much pedantic mistaking of notions for realities, of symbols and abstractions for the data of immediate experience. But these errors, however regrettable, do not do much harm, at any rate directly – though it sometimes happens that bad philosophical systems may do harm indirectly, by being used as justification for senseless and inhuman actions. It is in the social sphere, in the realm of politics and economics, that the Will of Order becomes really dangerous.

Here the theoretical reduction of unmanageable multiplicity to comprehensible unity becomes the practical reduction of human diversity to subhuman uniformity, of freedom to servitude. In politics the equivalent of a fully developed scientific theory or philosophical system is a totalitarian dictatorship. In economics, the equivalent of a beautifully composed work of art is the smoothly running factory in which the workers are perfectly adjusted to the machines. The Will to Order can make tyrants out of those who merely aspire to clear up a mess. The beauty of tidiness is used as a justification for despotism.

Organization is indispensable; for liberty arises and has meaning only within a self-regulating community of freely co-operating individuals. But, though indispensable, organization can also be fatal. Too much organization transforms men and women into automata, suffocates the creative spirit and abolishes the very possibility of freedom. As usual, the only safe course is in the middle, between the extremes of *laissez-faire* at one end of the scale and of total control at the other.

During the past century the successive advances in technology have been accompanied by corresponding advances in organization. Complicated machinery has had to be matched by complicated social arrangements, designed to work as smoothly and efficiently as the new instruments of production. In order to fit into these organizations, individuals have had to de-individualize themselves, have had to deny their native diversity and conform to a standard pattern, have had to do their best to become automata.

The dehumanizing effects of over-organization are reinforced by the dehumanizing effects of overpopulation. Industry, as it expands, draws an ever greater proportion of humanity's increasing numbers into large cities. But life in large cities is not conducive to mental health (the highest incidence of schizophrenia, we are told, occurs among the swarming inhabitants of industrial slums); nor does it foster the kind of responsible freedom within small self-governing groups, which is the first condition of a genuine democracy. City life is anonymous and, as it were, abstract. People are related to one another, not as total personalities, but as the embodiments of economic functions or, when they are not at work, as irresponsible seekers of entertainment. Subjected to this kind of life, individuals tend to feel lonely and insignificant. Their existence ceases to have any point or meaning.

Biologically speaking, man is a moderately gregarious, not a completely social animal – a creature more like a wolf, let us say, or an elephant, than like a bee or an ant. In their original form human societies bore no resemblance to the hive or the ant heap; they were merely packs. Civilization is, among other things, the process by which primitive packs are transformed into an analogue, crude and mechanical, of the social insects' organic communities. At the present time the pressures of overpopulation and technological changes are accelerating this process. The termitary has come to seem a realizable and even, in some eyes, a desirable ideal. Needless to say, the ideal will never in fact be realized. A great gulf separates the social insects from the not too gregarious, big-brained mammal; and even though the mammal should do his best to imitate the insect, the gulf would remain. However hard they try, men cannot create a social organism, they can only create an organization. In the process of trying to create an organism they will merely create a totalitarian despotism.

Brave New World presents a fanciful and somewhat ribald picture of a society, in which the attempt to recreate human beings in the likeness of termites has been pushed almost to the limits of the possible. That we are being propelled in the direction of Brave New World is obvious. But no less obvious is the fact that we can, if we so desire, refuse to co-operate with the blind forces that are propelling us. For the moment, however, the wish to resist does not seem to be very strong or very widespread. As Mr William Whyte has shown in his remarkable book, *The Organization Man*, a new Social Ethic is replacing our traditional ethical system – the system in which the individual is primary. The key words in this Social Ethic are 'adjustment', 'adaptation', 'socially orientated behaviour', 'belongingness', 'acquisition of social skills', 'team work', 'group living', 'group loyalty', 'group dynamics', 'group thinking', 'group creativity'. Its basic assumption is that the social whole has greater worth and significance than its individual parts, that inborn biological differences should be sacrificed to cultural uniformity, that the rights of the collectivity take precedence over what the eighteenth century called the Rights of Man. According to the Social Ethic, Jesus was completely wrong in asserting that the Sabbath was made for man. On the contrary, man was made for the Sabbath, and must sacrifice his inherited idiosyncrasies and pretend to be the kind of standardized good mixer that organizers of group activity regard as ideal for their purposes. This ideal man is the man who displays 'dynamic conformity' (delicious phrase!) and an intense loyalty to the group, an unflagging desire to subordinate himself, to belong. And the ideal man must have an ideal wife, highly gregarious, infinitely adaptable and not merely resigned to the fact that her husband's first loyalty is to the Corporation, but actively loyal on her own account. 'He for God only,' as Milton said of Adam and Eve, 'she for God in him.' And in one important respect the wife of the ideal organization man is a good deal worse off than our First Mother. She and Adam were permitted by the Lord to be completely uninhibited in the matter of 'youthful dalliance'.

> Nor turned, I ween,
> Adam from his fair spouse, nor Eve the rites
> Mysterious of connubial love refused

Today, according to a writer in the *Harvard Business Review*, the wife of the man who is trying to live up to the ideal proposed by the Social Ethic, 'must not demand too much of her husband's time and interest. Because of his single-minded concentration on his job, even his sexual activity must be relegated to a secondary place.' The monk makes vows of poverty, obedience and chastity. The organization man is allowed to be rich, but promises obedience ('he accepts authority without resentment, he looks up to his super-iors' – *Mussolini ha sempre ragione)*and he must be prepared, for the greater glory of the organization that employs him, to forswear even conjugal love.*

It is worth remarking that, in *1984,* the members of the Party are compelled to conform to a sexual ethic of more than Puritan severity. In *Brave New World,* on the other hand, all are permitted to indulge their sexual impulses without let or hin-drance. The society described in Orwell's fable is a society permanently at war, and the aim of its rulers is first, of course, to exercise power for its own delightful sake, and second, to keep their subjects in that state of constant tension which a state of constant war demands of those who wage it. By crusading against sexuality the bosses are able to maintain the required tension in their lust for power in a most gratifying way. The society described in *Brave New World* is a world-state in which war has been eliminated and where the first aim of the rulers is at all cost to keep their subjects from making trouble. This they achieve by (among other methods) legalizing a degree of

---

* Under Mao Tse-tung these capitalistic counsels of perfection have become commandments and been modified as regulations. In the new People's Communes the conjugal state has been abolished. That there may be no mutual tenderness, husbands and wives are housed in separate barracks and are permitted to sleep together (for a brief hour or two, like prostitutes and their clients) only on alternate Saturday nights.

sexual freedom (made possible by the abolition of the family) that practically guarantees the Brave New Worlders against any form of destructive (or creative) emotional tension. In *1984* the lust for power is satisfied by inflicting pain; in *Brave New World,* by inflicting a hardly less humiliating pleasure.

The current Social Ethic, it is obvious, is merely a justification after the fact of the less desirable consequences of over-organization. It represents a pathetic attempt to make a virtue of necessity, to extract a positive value from an unpleasant datum. It is a very unrealistic, and therefore very dangerous, system of morality. The social whole, whose value is assumed to be greater than that of its component parts, is not an organism in the sense that a hive or a termitary may be thought of as an organism. It is merely an organization, a piece of social machinery. There can be no value except in relation to life and awareness. An organization is neither conscious nor alive. Its value is instrumental and derivative. It is not good in itself; it is good only to the extent that it promotes the good of the individuals who are the parts of the collective whole. To give organizations precedence over persons is to subordinate ends to means. What happens when ends are subordinated to means was clearly demonstrated by Hitler and Stalin. Under their hideous rule personal ends were subordinated to organizational means by a mixture of violence and propaganda, systematic terror and the systematic manipulation of minds. In the more efficient dictatorships of tomorrow there will probably be much less violence than under Hitler and Stalin. The future dictator's subjects will be painlessly regimented by a corps of highly trained Social Engineers. 'The challenge of social engineering in our time,' writes an enthusiastic advocate of this new science, 'is like the challenge of technical engineering fifty years ago. If the first half of the twentieth century was the era of the technical engineers, the second half may well be the era of the social engineers' – and the twenty-first century, I suppose, will be the era of World Controllers, the scientific caste system and Brave New World. To the question *quis custodiet custodes?* – who will mount guard over our guardians, who will engineer the engineers? – the answer is a bland denial that they need any supervision. There seems to be a touching belief among certain Ph.D.s in sociology that Ph.D.s in sociology will never be corrupted by power. Like Sir Galahad's, their strength is as the strength of ten because they are scientists and have taken six thousand hours of social studies.

Alas, higher education is not necessarily a guarantee of higher virtue, or higher political wisdom. And to these misgivings on ethical and psychological grounds must be added misgivings of a purely scientific character. Can we accept the theories on which the social engineers base their practice, and in terms of which they justify their manipulations of human beings? For example, Professor Elton Mayo tells us categorically that 'man's desire to be continuously associated in work with his fellows is a strong, if not the strongest human characteristic'. This, I would say, is manifestly untrue. Some people have the kind of desire described by Mayo; others do not. It is a matter of temperament and inherited constitution. Any social organization based upon the assumption that 'man' (whoever 'man' may be) desires to be continuously associated with his fellows would be, for many individual men and women, a bed of Procrustes. Only by being amputated or stretched upon a rack could they be adjusted to it.

Again, how romantically misleading are the lyrical accounts of the Middle Ages, with which many contemporary theorists of social relations adorn their works! 'Membership in a guild, manorial estate or village protected medieval man throughout his life and gave him peace and serenity.' Protected him from what, we may ask? Certainly not from remorseless bullying at the hands of his superiors. And along with all that 'peace and serenity' there was, throughout the Middle Ages, an enormous amount of chronic frustration, acute unhappiness and a passionate resentment against the rigid, hierarchical system that permitted no vertical movement up the social ladder and, for those who were bound to the land, very little horizontal movement in space. The impersonal forces of overpopulation and over-organization, and the social engineers who are trying to direct these forces, are pushing us in the direction of a new medieval system. This revival will be made more acceptable than the original by such Brave-New-Worldian amenities as infant conditioning, sleep teaching and drug-induced euphoria; but, for the majority of men and women, it will still be a kind of servitude.

IV

Propaganda in a Democratic Society

'The doctrines of Europe', Jefferson wrote, 'were that men in numerous associations cannot be restrained within the limits of order and justice, except by forces physical and moral wielded over them by authorities independent of their will . . . We (the founders of the New American democracy) believe that man was a rational animal, endowed by nature with rights, and with an innate sense of justice, and that he could be restrained from wrong, and protected in right, by moderate powers, confided to persons of his own choice and held to their duties by dependence on his own will.' To post-Freudian ears, this kind of language seems touchingly quaint and ingenuous. Human beings are a good deal less rational and innately just than the optimists of the eighteenth century supposed. On the other hand they are neither so morally blind nor so hopelessly unreasonable as the pessimists of the twentieth would have us believe. In spite of the Id and the Unconscious, in spite of endemic neurosis and the prevalence of low IQ's, most men and women are probably decent enough and sensible enough to be trusted with the direction of their own destinies.

Democratic institutions are devices for reconciling social order with individual freedom and initiative, and for making the immediate power of a country's rulers subject to the ultimate power of the ruled. The fact that, in Western Europe and America, these devices have worked, all things considered, not too badly is proof enough that the eighteenth-century optimists were not entirely wrong. Given a fair chance, human beings can govern themselves, and govern themselves better, though perhaps with less mechanical efficiency, than they can be governed by 'authorities independent of their will'. Given a fair chance, I repeat; for the fair chance is an indispensable pre-requisite. No people that passes abruptly from a state of subservience under the rule of a despot to the completely unfamiliar state of political independence can be said to have a fair chance of making democratic institutions work. Again, no people in a precarious economic condition has a fair chance of being able to govern itself democratically. Liberalism flourishes in an atmosphere of prosperity and declines as declining prosperity makes it necessary for the government to intervene ever more frequently and drastically in the affairs of its subjects. Overpopulation and over-organization are two conditions which, as I have already pointed out, deprive a society of a fair chance of making democratic institutions work effectively. We see, then, that there are certain historical, economic, demographic and technological conditions which make it very hard for Jefferson's rational animals, endowed by nature with inalienable rights and an innate sense of justice, to exercise their reason, claim their rights and act justly within a democratically organized society. We in the West have been supremely fortunate in having been given our fair chance of making the great experiment in self-government. Unfortunately it now looks as though, owing to recent changes in our circumstances, this infinitely precious fair chance were being, little by little, taken away from us. And this, of course, is not the whole story. These blind impersonal forces are not the only enemies of individual liberty and democratic institutions. There are also forces of another, less abstract character, forces that can be deliberately used by power-seeking individuals whose aim is to establish partial or complete control over their fellows. Fifty years ago, when I was a boy, it seemed completely self-evident that the bad old days were over, that torture and massacre, slavery, and the persecution of heretics, were things of the past. Among people who wore top hats, travelled in trains, and took a bath every morning such horrors were simply out of the question. After all we were living in the twentieth century. A few years later these people who took daily baths and went to church in top hats were committing

atrocities on a scale undreamed of by the be-
nighted Africans and Asiatics. In the light of
recent history it would be foolish to suppose that
this sort of thing cannot happen again. It can and,
no doubt, it will. But in the immediate future
there is some reason to believe that the punitive
methods of *1984* will give place to the reinforce-
ments and manipulations of Brave New World.

There are two kinds of propaganda – rational
propaganda in favour of action that is consonant
with the enlightened self-interest of those who
make it and those to whom it is addressed, and
non-rational propaganda that is not consonant
with anybody's enlightened self-interest, but is
dictated by, and appeals to, passions, blind impulses, unconscious cravings or fears. Where the
actions of individuals are concerned, there are
motives more exalted than enlightened self-interest, but where collective action has to be taken in
the fields of politics and economics, enlightened
self-interest is probably the highest of effective
motives. If politicians and their constituents always acted to promote their own or their country's long-range self-interest, this world would be
an earthly paradise. As it is, they often act against
their own interests, merely to gratify their least
creditable passions; the world, in consequence, is
a place of misery. Propaganda in favour of action
that is consonant with enlightened self-interest
appeals to reason by means of logical arguments

based upon the best available evidence fully and honestly set forth. Propaganda in favour of action dictated by the impulses that are below self-interest, offers false, garbled or incomplete evidence, avoids logical argument and seeks to influence its victims by the mere repetition of catchwords, by the furious denunciation of foreign or domestic scapegoats, and by cunningly associating the lowest passions with the highest ideals, so that atrocities are perpetrated in the name of God and the most cynical kind of *realpolitik* becomes a matter of religious principle and patriotic duty.

In John Dewey's words, 'a renewal of faith in common human nature, in its potentialities in general, and in its power in particular to respond to reason and truth, is a surer bulwark against totalitarianism than a demonstration of material success or a devout worship of special legal and political forms'. The power to respond to reason and truth exists in all of us. But so, unfortunately, does the tendency to respond to unreason and falsehood – particularly in those cases where the falsehood evokes some enjoyable emotion, or where the appeal to unreason strikes some answering chord in the primitve, subhuman depths of our being. In certain fields of activity men have learned to respond to reason and truth pretty consistently. The authors of learned articles do not appeal to the passions of their fellow scientists and technologists. They set forth what, to the best of their knowledge, is the truth about some particular aspect of reality, they use reason to explain the facts they have observed, and they support their points of view with arguments that appeal to reason in other people. All this is fairly easy in the fields of physical science and technology. It is much more difficult in the fields of politics and religion and ethics. Here the relevant facts often elude us. As for the meaning of the facts, that of course depends upon the particular system of ideas in terms of which you choose to interpret them. And these are not the only difficulties that confront the rational truth-seeker. In public and in private life, it often happens that there is simply no time to collect the relevant facts or to weigh their significance. We are forced to act on insufficient evidence and by a light considerably less steady than that of logic. With the best will in the world, we cannot always be completely truthful or consistently rational. All that is in our power is to be as truthful and rational as circumstances permit us to be, and to respond as well as we can to the limited truth and imperfect reasonings offered for our consideration by others.

'If a nation expects to be ignorant and free', said Jefferson, 'it expects what never was and never will be ... The people cannot be safe without information. Where the press is free, and every man able to read, all is safe.' Across the Atlantic another passionate believer in reason was thinking, about the same time, in almost precisely similar terms. Here is what John Stuart Mill wrote of his father, the utilitarian philosopher, James Mill. 'So complete was his reliance upon the influence of reason over the minds of mankind, whenever it is allowed to reach them, that he felt as if all would be gained, if the whole population were able to read, and if all sorts of opinions were allowed to be addressed to them by word or in writing, and if by the suffrage they could nominate a legislature to give effect to the opinions they had adopted.' *All is safe, all would be gained!* Once more we hear the note of eighteenth-century optimism. Jefferson it is true, was a realist as well as an optimist. He knew by bitter experience that the freedom of the press can be shamefully abused. 'Nothing', he declared 'can now be believed which is seen in a newspaper.' And yet, he insisted (and we can only agree with him), 'within the pale of truth, the press is a noble institution, equally the friend of science and civil liberty'. Mass communication, in a word, is neither good nor bad; it is simply a force and, like any other force, it can be used either well or ill. Used in one way, the press, the radio and the cinema are indispensable to the survival of democracy. Used in another way, they are among the most powerful weapons in the dictator's armoury. In the field of mass communications as in almost every other field of enterprise, technological progress has hurt the Little Man and helped the Big Man. As lately as fifty years ago, every democratic country could boast of a great number of small journals and local newspapers. Thousands of country editors expressed thousands of independent opinions. Somewhere or other almost anybody could get almost anything printed. Today the press is still legally free; but most of the little papers have disappeared. The cost of wood-pulp, of modern printing machinery and of syndicated news is too high for the Little Man. In the totalitarian East there is political censorship, and the media of mass communication are controlled by the State. In the democratic West there is economic censorship and the media of mass communication are controlled by members of the Power Elite. Censorship by rising costs and concentration of communication-power in the hands of a few big concerns is less objectionable than State ownership and government propaganda; but certainly it is not something of which a Jeffersonian democrat could possibly approve.

In regard to propaganda, the early advocates of universal literacy and a free press envisaged only two possibilities: the propaganda might be true, or it might be false. They did not foresee what in fact has happened, above all in our Western capitalist democracies – the development of a vast mass communications industry, concerned in the main neither with the true nor the false, but with the unreal, the more or less totally irrelevant. In a word, they failed to take into account man's almost infinite appetite for distractions.

In the past most people never got a chance of fully satisfying this appetite. They might long for distractions, but the distractions were not provided. Christmas came but once a year, feasts were 'solemn and rare', there were few readers and very little to read, and the nearest approach to a neighbourhood movie theatre was the parish church, where the performances, though frequent, were somewhat monotonous. For conditions even remotely comparable to those now prevailing we must return to imperial Rome, where the populace was kept in good humour by frequent, gratuitous doses of many kinds of entertainment – from poetical dramas to gladiatorial fights, from recitations of Virgil to all-out boxing, from concerts to military reviews and public executions. But even in Rome there was nothing like the non-stop distraction now provided by newspapers and magazines, by radio, television and the cinema. In *Brave New World* non-stop distractions of the most fascinating nature (the feelies, orgy-porgy, centrifugal bumblepuppy) are deliberately used as instruments of policy, for·the purpose of preventing people from paying too much attention to the realities of the social and political situation. The other world of religion is different from the other world of entertainment;

but they still resemble one another in being most decidedly 'not of this world'. Both are distractions and, if lived in too continuously, both can become, in Marx's phrase, 'the opium of the people' and so a threat to freedom. Only the vigilant can maintain their liberties, and only those who are constantly and intelligently on the spot can hope to govern themselves effectively by democratic procedures. A society, most of whose members spend a great part of their time not on the spot, not here and now and in the calculable future, but somewhere else, in the irrelevant other worlds of sport and soap opera, of mythology and metaphysical phantasy, will find it hard to resist the encroachments of those who would manipulate and control it.

In their propaganda, today's dictators rely for the most part on repetition suppression and rationalization – the repetition of catchwords which they wish to be accepted as true, the suppression of facts which they wish to be ignored, the arousal and rationalization of passions which may be used in the interests of the Party or the State. As the art and science of manipulation come to be better understood, the dictators of the future will doubtless learn to combine these techniques with the non-stop distractions which, in the West, are now threatening to drown in a sea of irrelevance the rational propaganda essential to the maintenance of individual liberty and the survival of democratic institutions.

V

Propaganda under a Dictatorship

At his trial after the Second World War, Hitler's Minister for Armaments, Albert Speer, delivered a long speech in which, with remarkable acuteness, he described the Nazi tyranny and analysed its methods. 'Hitler's dictatorship', he said, 'differed in one fundamental point from all its predecessors in history. It was the first dictatorship in the present period of modern technical development, a dictatorship which made complete use of all technical means for the domination of its own country. Through technical devices like the radio and the loud-speaker, eighty million people were deprived of independent thought. It was thereby possible to subject them to the will of one man . . . Earlier dictators needed highly qualified assistants even at the lowest level – men who could think and act independently. The totalitarian system in the period of modern technical development can dispense with such men; thanks to modern methods of communication, it is possible to mechanize the lower leadership. As a result of this there has arisen the new type of the uncritical recipient of orders.'

In the Brave New World of my prophetic fable

technology had advanced far beyond the point it had reached in Hitler's day; consequently the recipients of orders were far less critical than their Nazi counterparts, far more obedient to the order-giving élite. Moreover they had been genetically standardized and post-natally conditioned to perform their subordinate functions, and could therefore be depended upon to behave almost as predictably as machines. As we shall see in a later chapter, this conditioning of 'the lower leadership' is already going on under the Communist dictatorships. The Chinese and the Russians are not relying merely on the indirect effects of advancing technology; they are working directly on the psycho-physical organisms of their lower leaders, subjecting minds and bodies to a system of ruthless and, from all accounts, highly effective conditioning. 'Many a man', said Speer, 'has been haunted by the nightmare that one day nations might be dominated by technical means. That nightmare was almost realized in Hitler's totalitarian system.' Almost, but not quite. The Nazis did not have time – and perhaps did not have the intelligence and the necessary knowledge – to brainwash and condition their lower leadership. This, it may be, is one of the reasons why they failed.

Since Hitler's day the armoury of technical devices at the disposal of the would-be dictator has been considerably enlarged. As well as the radio, the loud-speaker, the moving picture camera and the rotary press, the contemporary propagandist can make use of television to broadcast the image as well as the voice of his client, and can record both image and voice on spools of magnetic tape. Thanks to technological progress, Big Brother can now be almost as omnipresent as God. Nor is it only on the technical front that the hand of the would-be dictator has been strengthened. Since Hitler's day a great deal of work has been carried out in those fields of applied psychology and neurology which are the special province of the propagandist, the indoctrinator and the brainwasher. In the past these specialists in the art of changing people's minds were empiricists. By a method of trial and error they had worked out a number of techniques and procedures, which they used very effectively without, however, knowing precisely why they were effective. Today the art of mind-control is in process of becoming a science. The practitioners of this science know what they are doing and why. They are guided in their work by theories and hypotheses solidly established on a massive foundation of experimental evidence. Thanks to the new insights and the new techniques made possible by these insights, the nightmare that was 'all but realized in Hitler's totalitarian system' may soon be completely realizable.

But before we discuss these new insights and

techniques let us take a look at the nightmare that
so nearly came true in Nazi Germany. What were
the methods used by Hitler and Goebbels for
'depriving eighty million people of independent
thought and subjecting them to the will of one
man'? And what was the theory of human nature
upon which those terrifyingly successful methods
were based? These questions can be answered, for
the most part, in Hitler's own words. And what
remarkably clear and astute words they are!
When he writes about such vast abstractions as
Race History and Providence, Hitler is strictly
unreadable. But when he writes about the German masses and the methods he used for dominating and directing them, his style changes.
Nonsense gives place to sense, bombast to a
hard-boiled and cynical lucidity. In his philosophical lucubrations Hitler was either cloudily
day-dreaming or reproducing other people's half-
baked notions. In his comments on crowds and
propaganda he was writing of things he knew by
first-hand experience. In the words of his ablest
biographer, Mr Alan Bullock, 'Hitler was the
greatest demagogue in history. Those who add,
"only a demagogue", fail to appreciate the nature
of political power in an age of mass politics. As he
himself said, "To be a leader means to be able to
move the masses."' Hitler's aim was first to move
the masses and then, having pried them loose
from their traditional loyalties and moralities, to

impose upon them (with the hypnotized consent of the majority) a new authoritarian order of his own devising. 'Hitler', wrote Hermann Rauschning in 1939, 'has a deep respect for the Catholic church and the Jesuit order; not because of their Christian doctrine, but because of the "machinery" they have elaborated and controlled, their hierarchical system, their extremely clever tactics, their knowledge of human nature and their wise use of human weakness in ruling over believers.' Ecclesiasticism without Christianity, the discipline of a monastic rule, not for God's sake or in order to achieve personal salvation, but for the sake of the State and for the greater glory and power of the demagogue turned Leader – this was the goal towards which the systematic moving of the masses was to lead.

Let us see what Hitler thought of the masses he moved and how he did the moving. The first principle from which he started was a value judgment: the masses are utterly contemptible. They are incapable of abstract thinking and uninterested in any fact outside the circle of their immediate experience. Their behaviour is determined, not by knowledge and reason, but by feelings and unconscious drives. It is in these drives and feelings that 'the roots of their positive as well as their negative attitudes are implanted'. To be successful a propagandist must learn how to manipulate these instincts and emotions. 'The driving force which has brought about the most tremendous revolutions on this earth has never been a body of scientific teaching which has gained power over the masses, but always a devotion which has inspired them, and often a kind of hysteria which has urged them into action. Whoever wishes to win over the masses must know the key that will open the door of their hearts.' – In post-Freudian jargon, of their unconscious.

Hitler made his strongest appeal to those members of the lower middle classes who had been ruined by the inflation of 1923, and then ruined all over again by the depression of 1929 and the following years. 'The masses' of whom he speaks were these bewildered, frustrated and chronically anxious millions. To make them more mass-like, more homogeneously subhuman, he assembled them, by the thousands and the tens of thousands, in vast halls and arenas, where individuals could lose their personal identity, even their elementary humanity and be merged with the crowd. A man or woman makes direct contact with society in two ways: as a member of some familial, professional or religious group, or as a member of a crowd. Groups are capable of being as moral and intelligent as the individuals who form them; a crowd is chaotic, has no purpose of its own, and is capable of anything except intelligent action and realistic thinking. Assembled in a crowd, people lose their powers of reasoning and their capacity for moral choice. Their suggestibility is increased to the point where they cease to have any judgment or will of their own. They become very excitable, they lose all sense of individual or collective responsibility, they are subject to sudden accesses of rage, enthusiasm and panic. In a word, a man in a crowd behaves as though he had swallowed a large dose of some powerful intoxicant. He is a victim of what I have called 'herd-poisoning'. Like alcohol, herd-poison is an active, extraverted drug. The crowd-intoxicated individual escapes from responsibility, intelligence and morality into a kind of frantic, animal mindlessness.

During his long career as an agitator, Hitler had studied the effects of herd-poison and had learned how to exploit them for his own purposes. He had discovered that the orator can appeal to those 'hidden forces', which motivate men's actions, much more effectively than can the writer. Reading is a private, not a collective activity. The writer speaks only to individuals, sitting by themselves in a state of normal sobriety. The orator speaks to masses of individuals, already well primed with herd-poison. They are at his mercy and, if he knows his business, he can do what he likes with them. As an orator, Hitler knew his business supremely well. He was able, in his own words, 'to follow the lead of the great mass in such a way that from the living emotion of his hearers the apt word which he needed would be suggested to him and in its turn this would go straight to the heart of his hearers'. Otto Strasser called him 'a loud-speaker, proclaiming the most secret desires, the least admissible instincts, the sufferings and personal revolts of a whole nation'. Twenty years before Madison Avenue embarked upon 'Motivational Research', Hitler was systematically exploring and exploiting the secret fears and hopes, the cravings, anxieties and frustrations of the German masses. It is by manipulating 'hidden forces' that the advertising experts induce us to buy their wares – a toothpaste, a brand of cigarettes, a political candidate. And it was by appealing to the same hidden forces – and to others too dangerous for Madison Avenue to meddle with – that Hitler induced the German masses to buy themselves a Fuehrer, an insane philosophy and the Second World War.

Unlike the masses, intellectuals have a taste for rationality and an interest in facts. Their critical habit of mind makes them resistant to the kind of propaganda that works so well on the majority. Among the masses 'instinct is supreme, and from instinct comes faith . . . While the healthy common folk instinctively close their ranks to form a community of the people' (under a Leader, it goes without saying) 'intellectuals run this way and that, like hens in a poultry yard. With them one cannot make history; they cannot be used as elements composing a community.' Intellectuals are the kind of people who demand evidence and are shocked by logical inconsistencies and fallacies. They regard oversimplification as the original sin of the mind and have no use for the slogans, the unqualified assertions and sweeping generalizations which are the propagandist's stock in trade. 'All effective propaganda', Hitler wrote, 'must be confined to a few bare necessities and then must be expressed in a few stereotyped formulas.' These stereotyped formulas must be constantly repeated for 'only constant repetition will finally succeed in imprinting an idea upon the memory of a crowd'. Philosophy teaches us to feel uncertain about the things that seem to us self-evident. Propaganda, on the other hand, teaches us to accept as self-evident matters about which it would be reasonable to suspend our judgment or to feel doubt. The aim of the demagogue is to create social coherence under his own leadership. But, as Bertrand Russell has pointed out, 'systems of dogma without empirical foundations, such as scholasticism, Marxism and fascism, have the advantage of producing a great deal of social coherence among their disciples'. The demagogic propagandist must therefore be consistently dogmatic. All his statements are made without qualification. There are no greys in his picture of the world; everything is either diabolically black or celestially white. In Hitler's words, the propagandist should adopt 'a systematically one-sided attitude towards every problem that has to be dealt with'. He must never admit that he might be wrong or that people with a different point of view might be even partially right. Opponents should not be argued with; they should be attacked, shouted down, or, if they become too much of a nuisance, liquidated. The morally squeamish intellectual may be shocked by this kind of thing. But the masses are always convinced that 'right is on the side of the active aggressor'.

Such, then, was Hitler's opinion of humanity in the mass. It was a very low opinion. Was it also an incorrect opinion? The tree is known by its fruits, and a theory of human nature which inspired the kind of techniques that proved so horribly effective must contain at least an element of truth. Virtue and intelligence belong to human beings as individuals freely associating with other individuals in small groups. So do sin and stupidity. But the subhuman mindlessness to which the demagogue makes his appeal, the moral imbecility on which he relies when he goads his victims into action, are characteristics not of men and women as individuals, but of men and women in masses. Mindlessness and moral idiocy are not characteristically human attributes; they are symptoms of herd-poisoning. In all the world's higher religions, salvation and enlightenment are for individuals. The kingdom of heaven is within the mind of a person, not within the collective mindlessness of a crowd. Christ promised to be present where two or three are gathered together. He did not say anything about being present where thousands are intoxicating one another with herd-poison. Under the Nazis, enormous numbers of people were compelled to spend an enormous amount of time marching in serried ranks from point A to point B and back again to point A. 'This keeping of the whole population on the march seemed to be a senseless waste of time and energy. Only much later', adds Hermann Rauschning, 'was there revealed in it a subtle intention based on a well-judged adjustment of ends and means. Marching diverts men's thoughts. Marching kills thought. Marching makes an end of individuality. Marching is the indispensable magic stroke performed in order to accustom the people to a mechanical, quasi-ritualistic activity until it becomes second nature.'

From his point of view and at the level where he had chosen to do his dreadful work, Hitler was perfectly correct in his estimate of human nature. To those of us who look at men and women as individuals rather than as members of crowds, or of regimented collectives, he seems hideously wrong. In an age of accelerating overpopulation, of accelerating over-organization and ever more efficient means of mass communication, how can we preserve the integrity and re-assert the value of the human individual? This is a question that can still be asked and perhaps effectively answered. A generation from now it may be too late to find an answer and perhaps impossible, in the stifling collective climate of that future time, even to ask the question.

VI

The Arts of Selling

The survival of democracy depends on the ability of large numbers of people to make realistic choices in the light of adequate information. A dictatorship, on the other hand, maintains itself by censoring or distorting the facts, and by appealing, not to reason, not to enlightened self-interest, but to passion and prejudice, to the powerful 'hidden forces', as Hitler called them, present in the unconscious depths of every human mind.

In the West, democratic principles are proclaimed and many able and conscientious publicists do their best to supply electors with adequate information and to persuade them, by rational argument, to make realistic choices in the light of that information. All this is greatly to the good. But unfortunately propaganda in the Western democracies, above all in America, has two faces and a divided personality. In charge of the editorial department there is often a democratic Dr Jekyll – a propagandist who would be very happy to prove that John Dewey had been right about the ability of human nature to respond to truth and reason. But this worthy man controls only a part of the machinery of mass communication. In charge of advertising we find an anti-democratic, because anti-rational, Mr Hyde – or rather a Doctor Hyde, for Hyde is now a Ph.D. in psychology and has a master's degree as well in the Social Sciences. This Dr Hyde would be very unhappy indeed if everybody always lived up to John Dewey's faith in human nature. Truth and reason are Jekyll's affairs, not his. Hyde is a Motivation Analyst, and his business is to study human weaknesses and failings, to investigate those unconscious desires and fears by which so much of men's conscious thinking and overt doing is determined. And he does this, not in the spirit of the moralist who would like to make people better, or of the physician who would like to improve health, but simply in order to find out the best way to take advantage of their ignorance and to exploit their irrationality for the pecuniary benefit of his employers. But after all, it may be argued, 'capitalism is dead, consumerism is king' – and consumerism requires the services of expert salesmen versed in all the arts (including the more insidious arts) of persuasion. Under a free enterprise system commercial propaganda by any and every means is absolutely indispensable. But the indispensable is not necessarily the desirable. What is demonstrably good in the sphere of economics may be far from good for men and women as voters or even as human beings. An earlier, more moralistic generation would have been profoundly shocked by the bland cynicism of the Motivation Analysts. Today we read a book like Mr Vance Packard's *The Hidden Persuaders*, and are more amused than horrified, more resigned than indignant. Given Freud, given Behaviourism, given the mass producer's chronically desperate need for mass consumption, this is the sort of thing that is only to be expected. But what, we may ask, is the sort of thing that is to be expected in the future? Are Hyde's activities compatible in the long run with Jekyll's? Can a campaign in favour of rationality be successful in the teeth of another and even more vigorous campaign in favour of irrationality? These are questions which, for the moment, I shall not attempt to answer, but shall leave hanging, so to speak, as a backdrop to our discussion of the methods of mass persuasion in a technologically advanced democratic society.

The task of the commercial propagandist in a democracy is in some ways easier and in some ways more difficult than that of a political propagandist employed by an established dictator or a dictator in the making. It is easier in as much as almost everyone starts out with a prejudice in favour of beer, cigarettes and refrigerators, whereas almost nobody starts out with a prejudice in favour of tyrants. It is more difficult in as much as the commercial propagandist is not permitted, by the rules of his particular game, to appeal to the more savage instincts of his public. The advertiser of dairy products would dearly love to tell his readers and listeners that all their troubles are caused by the machinations of a gang of godless international margarine manufacturers, and that it is their patriotic duty to march out and burn the oppressors' factories. This sort of thing, however, is ruled out, and he must be content with a milder approach. But the mild approach is less exciting than the approach through verbal or physical violence. In the long run, anger and hatred are self-defeating emotions. But in the short run they pay high dividends in the form of psychological and even (since they release large quantities of adrenalin and noradrenalin) physiological satisfaction. People may start out with an initial prejudice against tyrants; but when tyrants or would-be tyrants treat them to adrenalin-releasing propaganda about the wickedness of their enemies – particularly of enemies weak enough to be persecuted – they are ready to follow him with enthusiasm. In his speeches Hitler kept repeating such words as 'hatred', 'force', 'ruthless', 'crush', 'smash'; and he would accompany these violent words with even more violent gestures. He would yell, he would scream, his veins would swell, his face would turn purple. Strong emotion (as every actor and dramatist knows) is in the highest degree contagious. Infected by the malignant frenzy of the orator, the audience would groan and sob and scream in an orgy of uninhibited passion. And these orgies were so enjoyable that most of those who had experienced them eagerly came back for more. Almost all of us long for peace and freedom; but very few of us have much enthusiasm for the thoughts, feelings and actions that make for peace and freedom. Conversely, almost nobody wants war or tyranny; but a great many people find an intense pleasure in the thoughts, feelings and actions that make for war and tyranny. These thoughts, feelings and actions are too dangerous to be exploited for commercial purposes. Accepting this handicap, the advertising man must do the best he can with the less intoxicating emotions, the quieter forms of irrationality.

Effective rational propaganda becomes possible only when there is a clear understanding, on the part of all concerned, of the nature of symbols and of their relations to the things and events symbolized. Irrational propaganda depends for its effectiveness on a general failure to understand the nature of symbols. Simple-minded people tend to equate the symbol with what it stands for, to attribute to things and events some of the qualities expressed by the words in terms of which the propagandist has chosen, for his own purposes, to talk about them. Consider a simple example. Most cosmetics are made of lanolin, which is a mixture of purified wool-fat and water beaten up into an emulsion. This emulsion has many valuable properties: it penetrates the skin, it does not become rancid, it is mildly antiseptic, and so forth. But the commercial propagandists do not speak about the genuine virtues of the emulsion. They give it some picturesquely voluptuous name, talk ecstatically and misleadingly about feminine beauty, and show pictures of gorgeous blondes nourishing their tissues with skin food. 'The cosmetic manufacturers', one of their number has written, 'are not selling lanolin, they are selling hope.' For this hope, this fraudulent implication of a promise that they will be transfigured, women will pay ten or twenty times the value of the emulsion which the propagandists have so skilfully related, by means of misleading symbols, to a deep-seated and almost universal feminine wish – the wish to be more attractive to members of the opposite sex. The principles underlying this kind of propaganda are extremely simple. Find some common desire, some widespread unconscious fear or anxiety; think about some way to relate this wish or fear to the product you have to sell; then build a bridge of verbal or pictorial symbols over which your customer can pass from fact to compensatory dream, and from the dream to the illusion that your product, when purchased, will make the dream come true. 'We no longer buy oranges, we buy vitality. We do not buy just a car, we buy prestige.' And so with all the rest. In toothpaste, for example, we buy, not a mere cleanser and antiseptic, but release from the fear of being sexually repulsive. In vodka and whisky we are not buying a protoplasmic poison which, in small doses, may depress the nervous system in a psychologically valuable way; we are buying friendliness and good fellowship, the warmth of Dingley Dell and the brilliance of the Mermaid Tavern. With our laxatives we buy the health of a Greek God, the radiance of one of Diana's nymphs. With the monthly best seller we acquire culture, the envy of our less literate neighbours and the respect of the sophisticated. In every case the motivation analyst has found some deep-seated wish or fear, whose energy can be used to move the consumer to part with cash and so, indirectly, to turn the wheels of industry. Stored in the minds and bodies of countless individuals, this potential energy is released by, and transmitted along, a line of symbols carefully laid out so as to by-pass rationality and obscure the real issue.

Sometimes the symbols take effect by being disproportionately impressive, haunting and fascinating in their own right. Of this kind are the rites and pomps of religion. These 'beauties of holiness' strengthen faith where it already exists and, where there is no faith, contribute to conversion. Appealing, as they do, only to the aesthetic sense, they guarantee neither the truth nor the ethical value of the doctrines with which they have been, quite arbitrarily, associated. As a matter of plain historical fact, the beauties of holiness have often been matched and indeed surpassed by the beauties of unholiness. Under Hitler, for example, the yearly Nuremberg rallies were masterpieces of ritual and theatrical art. 'I had spent six years in St Petersburg before the war in the best days of the old Russian ballet,' writes Sir Neville Henderson, the British ambassador to Hitler's Germany, 'but for grandiose beauty I have never seen any ballet to compare with the Nuremberg rally.' One thinks of Keats – 'beauty is truth, truth beauty'. Alas, the identity exists only on some ultimate, supra-mundane level. On the levels of politics and theology, beauty is perfectly compatible with nonsense and tyranny. Which is very fortunate; for if beauty were incompatible with nonsense and tyranny, there would be precious little art in the world. The masterpieces of painting, sculpture and architecture were produced as religious or political propaganda, for the greater glory of a god, a government or a priesthood. But most kings and priests have been despotic and all religions have been riddled with superstition. Genius has been the servant of tyranny and art has advertised the merits of the local cult. Time, as it passes, separates the good art from the bad metaphysics. Can we learn to make this separation, not after the event, but while it is actually taking place? That is the question.

In commercial propaganda the principle of the disproportionately fascinating symbol is clearly understood. Every propagandist has his Art Department, and attempts are constantly being made to beautify the billboards with striking posters, the advertising pages of magazines with lively drawings and photographs. There are no masterpieces; for masterpieces appeal only to a limited audience, and the commercial propagandist is out to captivate the majority. For him, the ideal is a moderate excellence. Those who like this not too good, but sufficiently striking, art may be expected to like the products with which it has been associated and for which it symbolically stands.

Another disproportionately fascinating symbol is the Singing Commercial. Singing Commercials are a recent invention; but the Singing Theological and the Singing Devotional – the hymn and the psalm – are as old as religion itself. Singing Militaries, or marching songs, are coeval with war, and Singing Patriotics, the precursors of our national anthems, were doubtless used to promote group solidarity, to emphasize the distinction between 'us' and 'them', by the wandering bands of paleolithic hunters and food gatherers. To most people music is intrinsically attractive. Moreover, melodies tend to ingrain themselves in the listener's mind. A tune will haunt the memory during the whole of a lifetime. Here, for example, is a quite uninteresting statement or value judgment. As it stands nobody will pay attention to it. But now set the words to a catchy and easily remembered tune. Immediately they become words of power. Moreover, the words will tend automatically to repeat themselves every time the melody is heard or spontaneously remembered. Orpheus has entered into an alliance with Pavlov – the power of sound with the conditioned reflex. For the commercial propagandist, as for his colleagues in the fields of politics and religion, music possesses yet another advantage. Nonsense which it would be shameful for a reasonable being to write, speak or hear spoken, can be sung or listened to by that same rational being with pleasure and even with a kind of intellectual conviction. Can we learn to separate the pleasure of singing or of listening to song from the all too human tendency to believe in the propaganda which the song is putting over? That again is the question.

Thanks to compulsory education and the rotary press, the propagandist has been able, for many years past, to convey his messages to virtually every adult in every civilized country. Today, thanks to radio and television he is in the happy position of being able to communicate even with unschooled adults and not yet literate children.

Children, as might be expected, are highly

susceptible to propaganda. They are ignorant of the world and its ways, and therefore completely unsuspecting. Their critical faculties are undeveloped. The youngest of them have not yet reached the age of reason and the older ones lack the experience on which their new-found rationality can effectively work. In Europe, conscripts used to be playfully referred to as 'cannon fodder'. Their little brothers and sisters have now become radio fodder and television fodder. In my childhood we were taught to sing nursery rhymes and, in pious households, hymns. Today the little ones warble the Singing Commercials. Which is better – 'Rheingold is my beer, the dry beer', or 'Hey diddle-diddle, the cat and the fiddle'? 'Abide with me' or 'You'll wonder where the yellow went, when you brush your teeth with Pepsodent'? Who knows?

'I don't say that children should be forced to harass their parents into buying products they've seen advertised on television, but at the same time I cannot close my eyes to the fact that it's being done every day.' So writes the star of one of the many programmes beamed to a juvenile audience. 'Children', he adds, 'are living, talking records of what we tell them every day.' And in due course these living, talking records of television commercials will grow up, earn money and buy the products of industry. 'Think,' writes Mr Clyde Miller ecstatically, 'think of what it can mean to your firm in profits if you can condition a million or ten million children, who will grow up into adults trained to buy your product, as soldiers are trained in advance when they hear the trigger words, Forward March!' Yes, just think of it! And at the same time remember that the dictators and the would-be dictators have been thinking about this sort of thing for years, and that millions, tens of millions, hundreds of millions of children are in process of growing up to buy the local despot's ideological product and, like well-trained soldiers, to respond with appropriate behaviour to the trigger words implanted in those young minds by the despot's propagandists.

Self-government is in inverse ratio to numbers. The larger the constituency, the less value of any particular vote. When he is merely one of millions, the individual elector feels himself to be impotent, a negligible quantity. The candidates he has voted into office are far away, at the top of the pyramid of power. Theoretically they are the servants of the people; but in fact it is the servants who give orders and the people, far off at the base of the great pyramid, who must obey. Increasing population and advancing technology have resulted in an increase in the number and complexity of organizations, an increase in the amount of power concentrated in the hands of officials and a corresponding decrease in the amount of control exercised by electors, coupled with a decrease in the public's regard for democratic procedures. Already weakened by the vast impersonal forces at work in the modern world, democratic institutions are now being undermined from within by the politicians and their propagandists.

Human beings act in a great variety of irrational ways, but all of them seem to be capable, if given a fair chance, of making a reasonable choice in the light of available evidence. Democratic institutions can be made to work only if all concerned do their best to impart knowledge and to encourage rationality. But today, in the world's most powerful democracy, the politicians and their propagandists prefer to make nonsense of democratic procedures by appealing almost exclusively to the ignorance and irrationality of the electors. 'Both parties', we were told in 1956 by the editor of a leading business journal, 'will merchandize their candidates and issues by the same methods that business has developed to sell goods. These include scientific selection of appeals and planned repetition ... Radio spot announcements and ads will repeat phrases with a planned intensity. Billboards will push slogans of proven power ... Candidates need, in addition to rich voices and good diction, to be able to look "sincerely" at the TV camera.'

The political merchandisers appeal only to the weaknesses of voters, never to their potential strength. They make no attempt to educate the masses into becoming fit for self-government; they are content merely to manipulate and exploit them. For this purpose all the resources of psychology and the social sciences are mobilized and set to work. Carefully selected samples of the electorate are given 'interviews in depth'. These interviews in depth reveal the unconscious fears and wishes most prevalent in a given society at the time of an election. Phrases and images aimed at allaying or, if necessary, enhancing these fears, at satisfying these wishes, at least symbolically, are then chosen by the experts, tried out on readers and audiences, changed or improved in the light of the information thus obtained. After which the political campaign is ready for the mass communicators. All that is now needed is money and a candidate who can be coached to look 'sincere'. Under the new dispensation, political principles and plans for specific action have come to lose most of their importance. The personality of the candidate and the way he is projected by the advertising experts are the things that really matter.

In one way or another, as vigorous he-man or kindly father, the candidate must be glamorous. He must also be an entertainer who never bores his audience. Inured to television and radio, that audience is accustomed to being distracted and does not like to be asked to concentrate or make a prolonged intellectual effort. All speeches by the entertainer-candidate must therefore be short and snappy. The great issues of the day must be dealt with in five minutes at the most – and preferably (since the audience will be eager to pass on to something a little livelier than inflation or the H-bomb) in sixty seconds flat. The nature of oratory is such that there has always been a tendency among politicians and clergymen to over-simplify complex issues. From a pulpit or a platform even the most conscientious of speakers finds it very difficult to tell the whole truth. The methods now being used to merchandise the political candidate as though he were a deodorant, positively guarantee the electorate against ever hearing the truth about anything.

VII

Brainwashing

In the two preceding chapters I have described the techniques of what may be called wholesale mind-manipulation, as practised by the greatest demagogue and the most successful salesmen in recorded history. But no human problem can be solved by wholesale methods alone. The shotgun has its place, but so has the hypodermic syringe. In the chapters that follow I shall describe some of the more effective techniques for manipulating not crowds, not entire publics, but isolated individuals.

In the course of his epoch-making experiments on the conditioned reflex, Ivan Pavlov observed that, when subjected to prolonged physical or psychic stress, laboratory animals exhibit all the symptoms of a nervous breakdown. Refusing to cope any longer with the intolerable situation, their brains go on strike, so to speak, and either stop working altogether (the dog loses consciousness), or else resort to slowdowns and sabotage (the dog behaves unrealistically, or develops the kind of physical symptoms which, in a human being, we would call hysterical). Some animals are more resistant to stress than others. Dogs possessing what Pavlov called a 'strong excitatory' constitution break down much more quickly than dogs of a merely 'lively' (as opposed to a choleric or agitated) temperament. Similarily 'weak inhibitory' dogs reach the end of their tether much sooner than do 'calm imperturbable' dogs. But even the most stoical dog is unable to resist indefinitely. If the stress to which he is subjected is sufficiently intense or sufficiently prolonged, he will end by breaking down as abjectly and as completely as the weakest of his kind.

Pavlov's findings were confirmed in the most distressing manner, and on a very large scale, during the two World Wars. As the result of a single catastrophic experience, or of a succession of terrors less appalling but frequently repeated, soldiers develop a number of disabling psychophysical symptoms. Temporary unconsciousness, extreme agitation, lethargy, functional blindness or paralysis, completely unrealistic responses to the challenge of events, strange reversals of lifelong patterns of behaviour – all the symptoms, which Pavlov observed in his dogs, re-appeared among the victims of what in the First World War was called 'shell shock', in the Second 'battle fatigue'. Every man, like every dog, has his own individual limit of endurance. Most men reach their limits after about thirty days of more or less continuous stress under the conditions of modern combat. The more than averagely susceptible

succumb in only fifteen days. The more than
averagely tough can resist for forty-five or even
fifty days. Strong or weak, in the long run all of
them break down. All, that is to say, of those who
are initially sane. For, ironically enough, the only
people who can hold up indefinitely under the
stress of modern war are psychotics. Individual
insanity is immune to the consequences of collective insanity.

The fact that every individual has his breaking
point has been known and, in a crude unscientific
way, exploited from time immemorial. In some
cases man's dreadful inhumanity to man has been
inspired by the love of cruelty for its own horrible
and fascinating sake. More often, however, pure
sadism was tempered by utilitarianism, theology
or reasons of state. Physical torture and other
forms of stress were inflicted by lawyers in order
to loosen the tongues of reluctant witnesses; by
clergymen in order to punish the unorthodox and
induce them to change their opinions; by secret
police to extract confessions from persons suspec-
ted of being hostile to the government. Under
Hitler, torture, followed by mass extermination,
was used on those biological heretics, the Jews.
For a young Nazi, a tour of duty in the Extermination Camps was (in Himmler's words) 'the best
indoctrination on inferior beings and the subhuman races'. Given the obsessional quality of the
Anti-Semitism which Hitler picked up as a young

man in the slums of Vienna, this revival of the methods employed by the Holy Office against heretics and witches was inevitable. But in the light of the findings of Pavlov and of the knowledge gained by psychiatrists in the treatment of war neuroses, it seems a hideous and grotesque anachronism. Stresses amply sufficient to cause a complete cerebral breakdown can be induced by methods which, though hatefully inhuman, fall short of physical torture.

Whatever may have happened in earlier years, it seems fairly certain that torture is not extensively used by the Communist police today. They draw their inspiration, not from the Inquisitor or the SS man, but from the physiologist and his methodically conditioned laboratory animals. For the dictator and his policemen, Pavlov's findings have important practical implications. If the central nervous system of dogs can be broken down, so can the central nervous system of political prisoners. It is simply a matter of applying the right amount of stress for the right length of time. At the end of the treatment, the prisoner will be in a state of neurosis or hysteria, and will be ready to confess whatever his captors want him to confess.

But confession is not enough. A hopeless neurotic is no use to anyone. What the intelligent and practical dictator needs is not a patient to be institutionalized, or a victim to be shot, but a convert who will work for the Cause. Turning once again to Pavlov, he learns that, on their way to the point of final breakdown, dogs become more than normally suggestible. New behaviour patterns can easily be installed while the dog is at or near the limit of its cerebral endurance, and these new behaviour patterns seem to be ineradicable. The animal in which they have been implanted cannot be de-conditioned; that which it has learned under stress will remain an integral part of its make-up.

Psychological stresses can be produced in many ways. Dogs become disturbed when stimuli are unusually strong; when the interval between a stimulus and the customary response is unduly prolonged and the animal is left in a state of suspense; when the brain is confused by stimuli that run counter to what the dog has learned to expect; when stimuli make no sense within the victim's established frame of reference. Furthermore, it has been found that the deliberate induction of fear, rage or anxiety markedly heightens the dog's suggestibility. If these emotions are kept at a high pitch of intensity for a long enough time, the brain goes 'on strike'. When this happens, new behaviour patterns may be installed with the greatest of ease.

Among the physical stresses that increase a dog's suggestibility are fatigue, wounds and every form of sickness.

For the would-be dictator these findings possess important practical implications. They prove, for example that Hitler was quite right in maintaining that mass meetings at night were more effective than mass meetings in the day time. 'During the day', he wrote, 'man's will power revolts with highest energy against any attempt at being forced under another's will and another's opinion. In the evening, however, they succumb more easily to the dominating force of a stronger will.'

Pavlov would have agreed with him; fatigue increases suggestibility. (That is why, among other reasons, the commercial sponsors of television programmes prefer the evening hours and are ready to back their preferences with hard cash.)

Illness is even more effective than fatigue as an intensifier of suggestibility. In the past, sickrooms were the scene of countless religious conversions. The scientifically trained dictator of the future will have all the hospitals in his dominions wired for sound and equipped with pillow speakers. Canned persuasion will be on the air twenty-four hours a day, and the more important patients will be visited by political soul-savers and mind-changers just as, in the past, their ancestors were visited by priests, nuns and pious laymen.

The fact that strong negative emotions tend to heighten suggestibility and so facilitate a change of heart had been observed and exploited long be-

fore the days of Pavlov. As Dr William Sargant
has pointed out in his enlightening book, *Battle for
the Mind*, John Wesley's enormous success as a
preacher was based upon an intuitive understanding of the central nervous system. He would
open his sermon with a long and detailed descrip-
tion of the torments to which, unless they under-
went conversion, his hearers would undoubtedly
be condemned for all eternity. Then, when terror
and an agonizing sense of guilt had brought his
audience to the verge, or in some cases over the
verge, of a complete cerebral breakdown, he
would change his tone and promise salvation to
those who believed and repented. By this kind of
preaching, Wesley converted thousands of men,
women and children. Intense, prolonged fear
broke them down and produced a state of greatly
intensified suggestibility. In this state they were
able to accept the preacher's theological pronoun-
cements without question. After which they were
reintegrated by words of comfort, and emerged
from their ordeal with new and generally better
behaviour patterns ineradicably implanted in
their minds and nervous systems.

The effectiveness of political and religious
propaganda depends upon the methods employed, not upon the doctrines taught. These
doctrines may be true or false, wholesome or
pernicious – it makes little or no difference. If the
indoctrination is given in the right way at the

proper stage of nervous exhaustion, it will work. Under favourable conditions, practically everybody can be converted to practically anything.

We possess detailed descriptions of the methods used by the Communist police for dealing with political prisoners. From the moment he is taken into custody, the victim. is subjected systematically to many kinds of physical and psychological stress. He is badly fed, he is made extremely uncomfortable, he is not allowed to sleep for more than a few hours each night. And all the time he is kept in a state of suspension, uncertainty and acute apprehension. Day after day – or rather night after night, for these Pavlovian policemen understand the value of fatigue as an intensifier of suggestibility – he is questioned, often for many hours at a stretch, by interrogators who do their best to frighten, confuse and bewilder him. After a few weeks or months of such treatment, his brain goes on strike and he confesses whatever it is that his captors want him to confess. Then, if he is to be converted rather than shot, he is offered the comfort of hope. If he will but accept the true faith, he can yet be saved – not, of course, in the next life (for, officially, there is no next life), but in this.

Similar but rather less drastic methods were used during the Korean War on military prisoners. In their Chinese camps the young Western captives were systematically subjected to stress.

Thus, for the most trivial breaches of the rules, offenders would be summoned to the commandant's office, there to be questioned, browbeaten and publicly humiliated. And the process would be repeated, again and again, at any hour of the day or night. This continuous harassment produced in its victims a sense of bewilderment and chronic anxiety. To intensify their sense of guilt, prisoners were made to write and rewrite, in ever more intimate detail, long autobiographical accounts of their shortcomings. And after having confessed their own sins, they were required to confess the sins of their companions. The aim was to create within the camp a nightmarish society, in which everybody was spying on, and informing against, everyone else. To these mental stresses were added the physical stresses of malnutrition, discomfort and illness. The increased suggestibility thus induced was skilfully exploited by the Chinese, who poured into these abnormally receptive minds large doses of pro-Communist and anti-capitalist literature. These Pavlovian techniques were remarkably successful. One out of every seven American prisoners was guilty, we are officially told, of grave collaboration with the Chinese authorities, one out of three of technical collaboration.

It must not be supposed that this kind of treatment is reserved by the Communists exclusively for their enemies. The young field workers, whose business it was, during the first years of the new regime, to act as Communist missionaries and organizers in China's innumerable towns and villages were made to take a course of indoctrination far more intense than that to which any prisoner of war was ever subjected. In his *China under Communism* R. L. Walker describes the methods by which the party leaders are able to fabricate out of ordinary men and women the thousands of selfless fanatics required for spreading the Communist gospel and for enforcing Communist policies. Under this system of training, the human raw material is shipped to special camps, where the trainees are completely isolated from their friends, families and the outside world in general. In these camps they are made to perform exhausting physical and mental work; they are never alone, always in groups; they are encouraged to spy on one another; they are required to write self-accusatory autobiographies; they live in chronic fear of the dreadful fate that may befall them on account of what has been said about them by informers or of what they themselves have confessed. In this state of heightened suggestibility they are given an intensive course in theoretical and applied Marxism – a course in which failure to pass examinations may mean anything from ignominious expulsion to a term in a forced labour camp or even liquidation. After about six months of this kind of thing, prolonged mental and physical stress produces the results which Pavlov's findings would lead one to expect. One after another, or in whole groups, the trainees break down. Neurotic and hysterical symptoms make their appearance. Some of the victims commit suicide, others (as many, we are told, as twenty per cent of the total) develop a severe mental illness. Those who survive the rigours of the conversion process emerge with new and ineradicable behaviour patterns. All their ties with the past – friends, family, traditional decencies and pieties – have been severed. They are new men, re-created in the image of their new god and totally dedicated to his service.*

Throughout the Communist world tens of thousands of these disciplined and devoted young men are being turned out every year from hundreds of conditioning centres. What the Jesuits did for the Roman Church of the Counter-Reformation, these products of a more scientific and

* In the new People's Communes of China the educational methods hitherto reserved for missionaries are now being applied, it would seem, to everybody. A twelve-hour working day ensures a state of permanent exhaustion; spying, delation and ubiquitous policemen foster a chronic anxiety; and the forced repression of sexual impulses and the common affections tends to create a sense of profound and hopeless frustration. On men, women and children softened up by these tested Pavlovian methods there is poured a never ceasing stream of command and dogmatic assertion, of red-hot jingoism and hymns of hate, of threats of dire punishment mitigated by millennial promises of glorious things to come. How many millions will break down under this educational ordeal, remains to be seen.

even harsher training are now doing, and will doubtless continue to do, for the Communist Parties of Europe, Asia and Africa.

In politics Pavlov seems to have been an old-fashioned liberal. But, by a strange irony of fate, his researches and the theories he based upon them have called into existence a great army of fanatics dedicated heart and soul, reflex and nervous system, to the destruction of old-fashioned liberalism, wherever it can be found.

Brainwashing, as it is now practised, is a hybrid technique, depending for its effectiveness partly on the systematic use of violence, partly on skilful psychological manipulation. It represents the tradition of *1984* on its way to becoming the tradition of *Brave New World*. Under a long-established and well-regulated dictatorship our current methods of semi-violent manipulation will seem, no doubt, absurdly crude. Conditioned from earliest infancy (and perhaps also biologically predestined) the average middle- or lower-caste individual will never require conversion or even a refresher course in the true faith. The members of the highest caste will have to be able to think new thoughts in response to new situations: consequently their training will be much less rigid than the training imposed upon those whose business is not to reason why, but merely to do and die with the minimum of fuss. These upper-caste individuals will be members, still, of a wild species – the trainers and guardians, themselves only slightly conditioned, of a vast herd of completely domesticated animals. Their wildness will make it possible for them to become heretical and rebellious. When this happens they will have to be either liquidated, or brainwashed back into orthodoxy, or (as in *Brave New World*) exiled to some island, where they can give no further trouble, except of course to one another. But universal infant conditioning and the other techniques of manipulation and control are still a few generations away in the future. On the road to the Brave New World our rulers will have to rely on the transitional and provisional techniques of brainwashing.

VIII

Chemical Persuasion

In the Brave New World of my fables there was no whisky, no tobacco, no illicit heroin, no boot-legged cocaine. People neither smoked, nor drank, nor sniffed, nor gave themselves injections. Whenever anyone felt depressed or below par he would swallow a tablet or two of a chemical compound called Soma. The original Soma, from which I took the name of the hypothetical drug, was an unknown plant (possibly *Asclepias acida*) used by the ancient Aryan invaders of India in one of the most solemn of their religious rites. The intoxicating juice expressed from the stems of this plant was drunk by the priests and nobles in the course of an elaborate ceremony. In the Vedic hymns we are told that the drinkers of Soma were blessed in many ways. Their bodies were streng-thened, their hearts were filled with courage, joy and enthusiasm, their minds were enlightened, and in an immediate experience of eternal life they received the assurance of their immortality. But the sacred juice had its drawbacks. Soma was a dangerous drug – so dangerous that even the great sky-god, Indra, was sometimes made ill by drinking it. Ordinary mortals might even die of an overdose. But the experience was so transcendently blissful and enlightening that Soma drinking was regarded as a high privilege. For this privilege no price was too great.

The Soma of *Brave New World* had none of the drawbacks of its Indian original. In small doses it brought a sense of bliss, in larger doses it made you see visions and, if you took three tablets, you would sink in a few minutes into refreshing sleep. And all at no physiological or mental cost. The Brave New Worlders could take holidays from their black moods, or from the familiar annoyances of everyday life, without sacrificing their health or permanently reducing their efficiency.

In the Brave New World the Soma habit was not a private vice; it was a political institution, it was the very essence of the Life, Liberty and Pursuit of Happiness guaranteed by the Bill of Rights. But this most precious of the subjects' inalienable privileges was at the same time one of the most powerful instruments of rule in the dictator's armoury. The systematic drugging of individuals for the benefit of the State (and incidentally, of course, for their own delights) was a main plank in the policy of the World Controllers. The daily Soma ration was an insurance against personal maladjustment, social unrest and the spread of subversive ideas. Religion, Karl Marx declared, is the opium of the people. In the Brave New World this situation was reversed.

Opium, or rather Soma, was the people's religion. Like religion, the drug had power to console and compensate, it called up visions of another, better world, it offered hope, strengthened faith and promoted charity. 'Beer,' a poet has written,

> 'does more than Milton can
> To justify God's ways to man.'

And let us remember that, compared with Soma, beer is a drug of the crudest and most unreliable kind. In this matter of justifying God's ways to man, Soma is to alcohol as alcohol is to the theological arguments of Milton.

In 1931, when I was writing about the imaginary synthetic by means of which future generations would be made both happy and docile, the well-known American bio-chemist, Dr Irvine Page, was preparing to leave Germany, where he had spent the three preceding years at the Kaiser Wilhelm Institute, working on the chemistry of the brain. 'It is hard to understand', Dr Page has written in a recent article, 'why it took so long for scientists to get around to investigating the chemical reactions in their own brains. I speak', he adds, 'from acute personal experience. When I came home in 1931 . . . I could not get a job in this field (the field of brain chemistry) or stir a ripple of interest in it.' Today, twenty-seven years later, the non-existent ripple of 1931 has become a tidal wave of bio-chemical and psycho-pharmaco-logical research. The enzymes which regulate the workings of the brain are being studied. Within the body, hitherto unknown chemical substances such as adrenochrome and serotonin (of which Dr Page was a co-discoverer) have been isolated and their far-reaching effects on our mental and physical functions are now being investigated. Meanwhile new drugs are being synthesized – drugs that reinforce or correct or interfere with the actions of the various chemicals, by means of which the nervous system performs its daily and hourly miracles as the controller of the body, the instrument and mediator of consciousness. From our present point of view, the most interesting fact about these new drugs is that they temporarily alter the chemistry of the brain and the associated state of the mind without doing any permanent damage to the organism as a whole. In this respect they are like Soma – and profoundly unlike the mind-changing drugs of the past. For example, the classical tranquillizer is opium. But opium is a dangerous drug which, from neolithic times down to the present day, has been making addicts and ruining health. The same is true of the classical euphoric, alcohol – the drug which, in the words of the Psalm is, 'maketh glad the heart of man'. But unfortunately alcohol not only maketh glad the heart of man; it also, in excessive doses, causes illness and addiction, and has been a main source, for the last eight or ten thousand years, of crime, domestic unhappiness, moral degradation and avoidable accidents.

Among the classical stimulants, tea, coffee and maté are, thank goodness, almost completely harmless. They are also very weak stimulants. Unlike these 'cups that cheer but not inebriate', cocaine is a very powerful and a very dangerous drug. Those who make use of it must pay for their ecstasies, their sense of unlimited physical and mental power, by spells of agonizing depression, by such horrible physical symptoms as the sensation of being infested by myrjads of crawling insects, and by paranoid delusions that may lead to crimes of violence. Another stimulant of more recent vintage is amphetamine, better known under its trade name of Benzedrine. Amphetamine works very effectively – but works, if abused, at the expense of mental and physical health. It has been estimated that, in Japan, there are now about one million amphetamine addicts.

Of the classical vision-producers the best known are the peyote of Mexico and the South-Western United States and *Cannabis sativa*, consumed all over the world under such names as hashish, bhang, kif and marihuana. According to the best medical and anthropological evidence, peyote is far less harmful than the White Man's gin or whisky. It permits the Indians who use it in their religious rites to enter paradise, and to feel at one with the beloved community, without making them pay for the privilege by anything worse than the ordeal of having to chew on something with a revolting flavour and of feeling somewhat nauseated for an hour or two. *Cannabis sativa* is a less innocuous drug – though not nearly so harmful as the sensation-mongers would have us believe. The Medical Committee, appointed in 1944 by the Mayor of New York to investigate the problem of marihuana, came to the conclusion, after careful investigation, that *Cannabis sativa* is not a serious menace to society, or even to those who indulge in it. It is merely a nuisance.

From these classical mind-changers we pass to the latest products of psycho-pharmacological research. Most highly publicized of these are the three new tranquillizers, reserpine, chlorpromazine and meprobamate. Administered to certain classes of psychotics, the first two have proved to be remarkably effective, not in curing mental illness, but at least in temporarily abolishing their more distressing symptoms. Meprobamate (alias Miltown) produces similar effects in persons suffering from various forms of neurosis. None of these drugs is perfectly harmless; but their cost, in terms of physical health and mental efficiency, is extraordinarily low. In a world where nobody gets anything for nothing tranquillizers offer a great deal for very little. Miltown and chlorpromazine are not yet Soma; but they come fairly near to being one of the aspects of that mythical drug. They provide temporary relief from nervous tension without, in the great majority of cases, inflicting permanent organic harm, and without causing more than a rather slight impairment, while the drug is working, of intellectual and physical efficiency. Except as narcotics, they are probably to be preferred to the barbiturates, which blunt the mind's cutting edge and, in large doses, cause a number of undesirable psycho-physical symptoms and may result in a full-blown addiction.

In LSD-25 (lysergic acid diethylamide) the pharmacologists have recently created another aspect of Soma – a perception-improver and vision-producer that is, physiologically speaking, almost costless. This extraordinary drug, which is effective in doses as small as fifty or even twenty-five millionths of a gram, has power (like peyote) to transport people into the Other World. In the majority of cases, the Other World to which LSD-25 gives access is heavenly; alternatively it may be purgatorial or even infernal. But, positive or negative, the lysergic acid experience is felt by almost everyone who undergoes it to be profoundly significant and enlightening. In any event, the fact that minds can be changed so radically at so little cost to the body is altogether astonishing.

Soma was not only a vision-producer and a

tranquillizer; it was also (and no doubt imposs-
ibly) a stimulant of mind and body, a creator of
active euphoria as well as of the negative happiness that follows the release from anxiety and
tension.

The ideal stimulant – powerful but innocuous
– still awaits discovery. Amphetamine, as we
have seen, was far from satisfactory; it exacted too
high a price for what it gave. A more promising
candidate for the role of Soma in its third aspect is
Iproniazid, which is now being used to lift depressed patients out of their misery, to enliven the
apathetic and in general to increase the amount of
available psychic energy. Still more promising,
according to a distinguished pharmacologist of
my acquaintance, is a new compound, still in the
testing stage, to be known as Deaner. Deaner is
an amino-alcohol and is thought to increase the
production of acetyl-choline within the body, and
thereby to increase the activity and effectiveness
of the nervous system. The man who takes the
new pill needs less sleep, feels more alert and
cheerful, thinks faster and better – and all at next
to no organic cost, at any rate in the short run. It
sounds almost too good to be true.

We see then, that, though Soma does not yet
exist (and will probably never exist) fairly good
substitutes for the various aspects of Soma have
already been discovered. There are now physiologically cheap tranquillizers, physiologically cheap

vision-producers and physiologically cheap stimulants.

That a dictator could, if he so desired, make use of these drugs for political purposes is obvious. He could ensure himself against political unrest by changing the chemistry of his subjects' brains and so making them content with their servile conditions. He could use tranquillizers to calm the excited, stimulants to arouse enthusiasm in the indifferent, halluciants to distract the attention of the wretched from their miseries. But how, it may be asked, will the dictator get his subjects to take the pills that will make them think, feel and behave in the ways he finds desirable? In all probability it will be enough merely to make the pills available. Today alcohol and tobacco are available, and people spend considerably more on these very unsatisfactory euphorics, pseudo-stimulants and sedatives than they are ready to spend on the education of their children. Or consider the barbiturates and the tranquillizers. In the United States these drugs can be obtained only on a doctor's prescription. But the demand of the American public for something that will make life in an urban-industrial environment a little more tolerable is so great that doctors are now writing prescriptions for the various tranquillizers at the rate of forty-eight millions a year. Moreover, a majority of these prescriptions are re-filled. A hundred doses of happiness are not enough: send to the drugstore for another bottle – and, when that is finished for another . . . There can be no doubt that, if tranquillizers could be bought as easily and cheaply as aspirin, they would be consumed, not only by the billions, as they are at present, but by the scores and hundreds of billions. And a good, cheap stimulant would be almost as popular.

Under a dictatorship pharmacists would be instructed to change their tune with every change of circumstance. In times of national crisis it would be their business to push the sale of stimulants. Between crises, too much alertness and energy on the part of his subjects might prove embarrassing to the tyrant. At such times the masses would be urged to buy tranquillizers and vision-producers. Under the influence of these soothing syrups they could be relied upon to give their master no trouble.

As things now stand, the tranquillizers may prevent some people from giving enough trouble, not only to their rulers, but even to themselves. Too much tension is a disease; but so is too little. There are certain occasions when we *ought* to be tense, when an excess of tranquillity (and especially of tranquillity imposed from the outside, by a chemical) is entirely inappropriate.

At a recent symposium on meprobamate, in which I was a participant, an eminent bio-chemist playfully suggested that the United States

government should make a free gift to the Soviet
people of fifty billion doses of this most popular of
the tranquillizers. The joke had a serious point to
it. In a contest between two populations one of
which is being constantly stimulated by threats
and promises, constantly directed by one-pointed
propaganda, while the other is no less constantly
being distracted by television and tranquillized
by Miltown, which of the opponents is more likely
to come out on top?

As well as tranquillizing, hallucinating and
stimulating, the Soma of my fable had the power
of heightening suggestibility, and so could be used
to reinforce the effects of governmental propaganda. Less effectively and at a higher physiological cost, several drugs already in the pharmaco-
poeia can be used for the same purpose. There is
scopolamine, for example, the active principle of
henbane and, in large doses, a powerful poison;
there are pentothal and sodium amytal. Nick-
named for some odd reason 'the truth serum',
pentothal has been used by the police of various
countries for the purpose of extracting confessions
from (or perhaps suggesting confessions to) reluctant criminals. Pentothal and sodium amytal
lower the barrier between the conscious and the
subconscious mind and are of great value in the
treatment of 'battle fatigue' by the process known
in England as 'abreaction therapy', in America as
'narcosynthesis'. It is said that these drugs are

sometimes employed by the Communists when preparing important prisoners for their public appearance in court.

Meanwhile pharmacology, bio-chemistry and neurology are on the march, and we can be quite certain that, in the course of the next few years, new and better chemical methods for increasing suggestibility and lowering psychological resistance will be discovered. Like everything else, these discoveries may be used well or badly. They may help the psychiatrist in his battle against mental illness, or they may help the dictator in his battle against freedom. More probably (since science is divinely impartial) they will both enslave and make free, heal and at the same time destroy.

IX

Subconscious Persuasion

In a footnote appended to the 1919 edition of his book, *The Interpretation of Dreams*, Sigmund Freud called attention to the work of Dr Poetzl, an Austrian neurologist, who had recently published a paper describing his experiments with the tachistoscope. (The tachistoscope is an instrument that comes in two forms – a viewing box, into which the subject looks at an image that is exposed for a small fraction of a second; or a magic lantern with a high-speed shutter, capable of projecting an image very briefly upon a screen.) In these experiments 'Poetzl required the subjects to make a drawing of what they had consciously noted of a picture exposed to their view in a tachistoscope . . . He then turned his attention to the dreams dreamed by the subjects during the following night and required them once more to make drawings of appropriate portions of these dreams. It was shown unmistakably that those details of the exposed picture which had *not* been noted by the subject provided material for the construction of the dream.'

With various modifications and refinements Poetzl's experiments have been repeated several times, most recently by Dr Charles Fisher, who has contributed three excellent papers on the subject of dreams and 'pre-conscious perception' to the Journal of the American Psychoanalytic Association. Meanwhile the academic psychologists have not been idle. Confirming Poetzl's findings, their studies have shown that people actually see and hear a great deal more than they consciously know they see and hear, and that what they see and hear without knowing it is recorded by the subconscious mind and may affect their conscious thoughts, feelings and behaviour.

Pure science does not remain pure indefinitely. Sooner or later it is apt to turn into applied science and finally into technology. Theory modulates into industrial practice, knowledge becomes power, formulas and laboratory experiments undergo a metamorphosis, and emerge as the H-bomb. In the present case, Poetzl's nice little piece of pure science, and all the other nice little pieces of pure science in the field of pre-conscious perception, retained their pristine purity for a surprisingly long time. Then, in the early autumn of 1957, exactly forty years after the publication of Poetzl's original paper, it was announced that their purity was a thing of the past; they had been applied, they had entered the realm of technology. The announcement made a considerable stir, and was talked and written about all over the civilized world. And no wonder; for the new technique of 'subliminal projection', as it was called, was intimately associated with mass entertainment, and in the life of civilized human beings mass entertainment now plays a part comparable to that played, in the Middle Ages, by religion. Our epoch has been given many nicknames – the Age of Anxiety, the Atomic Age, the Space Age. It might, with equally good reason, be called the Age of Television Addiction, the Age of Soap Opera, the Age of the Disc Jockey. In such an age the announcement that Poetzl's pure science had been applied in the form of a technique of subliminal projection could not fail to arouse the most intense interest among the world's mass entertainees. For the new technique was aimed directly at them, and its purpose was to manipulate their minds without their being aware of what was being done to them. By means of specially designed tachistoscopes words or images were to be flashed for a millisecond or less upon the screens of television sets and motion picture theatres *during* (not before or after) the programme. 'Drink Coca-Cola' or 'Light up a Camel' would be superimposed upon the lovers' embrace, the tears of the broken- hearted mother, and the optic nerves of the viewers would record these secret messages, their subconscious minds would respond to them and in due course they would consciously feel a craving for soda pop and tobacco. And meanwhile other secret messages would be whispered too softly, or squeaked too shrilly, for conscious hearing. Consciously the listener might be paying attention to some such phrase as 'Darling, I love you'; but subliminally, beneath the threshold of awareness, his incredibly sensitive ears and his subconscious mind would be taking in the latest good news about deodorants and laxatives.

Does this kind of commercial propaganda really work? The evidence produced by the commercial firm that first unveiled a technique for subliminal projection was vague and, from a scientific point of view, very unsatisfactory. Repeated at regular intervals during the showing of a picture in a movie theatre, the command to buy more popcorn was said to have resulted in a fifty per cent increase in popcorn sales during the intermission. But a single experiment proves very little. Moreover this particular experiment was poorly set up. There were no controls and no attempt was made to allow for the many variables that undoubtedly affect the consumption of popcorn by a theatre audience. And anyhow was this the most effective way of applying the knowledge accumulated over the years by the scientific investigators of subconscious perception? Was it intrinsically probable that, by merely flashing the name of a product and a command to buy it, you would be able to break down sales resistance and recruit new customers? The answer to both these questions is pretty obviously in the negative. But this does not mean, of course, that the findings of the neurologists and psychologists are without any practical importance. Skilfully applied, Poetzl's nice little piece of pure science might well become a powerful instrument for the manipulation of unsuspecting minds.

For a few suggestive hints let us now turn from the popcorn vendors to those who, with less noise but more imagination and better methods, have been experimenting in the same field. In Britain, where the process of manipulating minds below the level of consciousness is known as 'strobonic injection', investigators have stressed the practical importance of creating the right psychological conditions for the subconscious persuasion. A suggestion above the threshold of awareness is more likely to take effect when the recipient is in a light hypnotic trance, under the influence of certain drugs, or has been debilitated by illness, starvation, or any kind of physical or emotional stress. But what is true for suggestions above the threshold of consciousness is also true for suggestions beneath that threshold. In a word, the lower the level of a person's psychological resistance, the greater will be the effectiveness of strobonically injected suggestions. The scientific dictator of tomorrow will set up his whispering machines and subliminal projectors in schools and hospitals (children and the sick are highly suggestible), and in all public places where audiences can be given a preliminary softening-up by suggestibility-increasing oratory or rituals.

From the conditions under which we may expect subliminal suggestion to be effective we now pass to the suggestions themselves. In what terms should the propagandist address himself to his victims' subconscious minds? Direct commands ('Buy popcorn' or 'Vote for Jones') and unqualified statements ('Socialism stinks' or 'X's toothpaste cures halitosis') are likely to take effect only upon those minds that are already partial to Jones and popcorn, already alive to the dangers of body odours and the public ownership of the means of production. But to strengthen existing faith is not enough; the propagandist, if he is worth his salt, must create new faith, must know how to bring the indifferent and the undecided over to his side, must be able to mollify and perhaps even convert the hostile. To subliminal assertion and command he knows that he must add subliminal persuasion.

Above the threshold of awareness, one of the most effective methods of non-rational persuasion is what may be called persuasion-by-association. The propagandist arbitrarily associates his chosen product, candidate or cause with some idea, some image of a person or thing, which most people, in a given culture, unquestioningly regard as good. Thus, in a selling campaign female beauty may be arbitrarily associated with anything from a bulldozer to a diuretic; in a political campaign patriotism may be associated with any cause from *apartheid* to integration, and with any kind of person, from a Mahatma Gandhi to a Senator McCarthy. Years ago, in Central America, I observed an example of persuasion-by-association which filled me with an appalled admiration for the men who had devised it. In the mountains of Guatemala the only imported art works are the coloured calendars distributed free of charge by the foreign companies whose products are sold to the Indians. The American calendars showed pictures of dogs, of landscapes, of young women in a state of partial nudity. But to the Indian dogs are merely utilitarian objects, landscapes are what he sees only too much of, every day of his life, and half-naked blondes are uninteresting, perhaps a little repulsive. American calendars were, in consequence, far less popular than German calendars; for the German advertisers had taken the trouble to find out what the Indians valued and were interested in. I remember in particular one masterpiece of commercial propaganda. It was a calendar put out by a manufacturer of aspirin. At the bottom of the picture one saw the familiar trademark on the familiar bottle of white tablets. Above it were no snow-scenes or autumnal woods, no cocker

spaniels or bosomy chorus girls. No – the wily
Germans had associated the pain-relievers with a
brightly coloured and extremely life-like picture
of the Holy Trinity sitting on a cumulus cloud
and surrounded by St Joseph, the Virgin Mary,
assorted saints and a large number of angels. The
miraculous virtues of acetyl salicylic acid were
thus guaranteed, in the Indians' simple and
deeply religious minds, by God the Father and
the entire heavenly host.

This kind of persuasion-by-association is something to which the techniques of subliminal projection seem to lend themselves particularly well.
In a series of experiments carried out at New
York University, under the auspices of the National Institution of Health, it was found that a
person's feelings about some consciously seen
image could be modified by associating it, on the
subconscious level, with another image, or, better
still, with value-bearing words. Thus, when associated, on the subconscious level, with the word
'happy', a blank expressionless face would seem
to the observer to smile, to look friendly, amiable,
outgoing. When the same face was associated,
also on the subconscious level, with the word
'angry', it took on a forbidding expression, and
seemed to the observer to have become hostile
and disagreeable. (To a group of young women, it
also came to seem very masculine – whereas
when it was associated with 'happy', they saw the

face as belonging to a member of their own sex. Fathers and husbands, please take note.) For the commercial and political propagandist, these findings, it is obvious, are highly significant. If he can put his victims into a state of abnormally high suggestibility, if he can show them, while they are in that state, the thing, the person or, through a symbol, the cause he has to sell, and if, on the subconscious level, he can associate this thing, person or symbol with some value-bearing word or image, he may be able to modify their feelings and opinions without their having any idea of what he is doing. It should be possible, according to an enterprising commercial group in New Orleans, to enhance the entertainment value of films and television plays by using this technique. People like to feel strong emotions and therefore enjoy tragedies, thrillers, murder mysteries and tales of passion. The dramatization of a fight or an embrace produces strong emotions in the spectators. It might produce even stronger emotions if it were associated, on the subconscious level, with appropriate words or symbols. For example, in the film version of *A Farewell to Arms*, the death of the heroine in childbirth might be made even more distressing than it already is by subliminally flashing upon the screen, again and again, during the playing of the scene, such ominous words as 'pain', 'blood' and 'death'. Consciously, the words would not be seen; but their effect upon the subconscious mind might be very great and these effects might powerfully reinforce the emotions evoked, on the conscious level, by the acting and the dialogue. If, as seems pretty certain, subliminal projection can consistently intensify the emotions felt by movie-goers, the motion picture industry may yet be saved from bankruptcy – that is, if the producers of television plays don't get there first.

In the light of what has been said about persuasion-by-association and the enhancement of emotions by subliminal suggestion, let us try to imagine what the political meeting of tomorrow will be like. The candidate (if there is still a question of candidates), or the appointed representative of the ruling oligarchy, will make his speech for all to hear. Meanwhile the tachistoscopes, the whispering and squeaking machines, the projectors of images so dim that only the subconscious mind can respond to them, will be reinforcing what he says by systematically associating the man and his cause with positively charged words and hallowed images, and by strobonically injecting negatively charged words and odious symbols whenever he mentions the enemies of the state or the party. In the United States brief flashes of Abraham Lincoln and the words 'government by the people' will be projected upon the rostrum. In Russia the speaker will, of course, be associated with glimpses of

Lenin, with the words 'people's democracy', with the prophetic beard of Father Marx. Because all this is still safely in the future, we can afford to smile. Ten or twenty years from now, it will probably seem a good deal less amusing. For what is now merely science fiction will have become everyday political fact.

Poetzl was one of the portents which, when writing *Brave New World*, I somehow overlooked. There is no reference in my fable to subliminal projection. It is a mistake of omission which, if I were to re-write the book today, I should most certainly correct.

X

Hypnopaedia

In the late autumn of 1957 the Woodland Road Camp, a penal institution in Tulare County, California, became the scene of a curious and interesting experiment. Miniature loud-speakers were placed under the pillows of a group of prisoners who had volunteered to act as psychological guinea-pigs. Each of these pillow speakers was hooked up to a phonograph in the Warden's office. Every hour throughout the night an inspirational whisper repeated a brief homily on 'the principles of moral living'. Waking at midnight, a prisoner might hear this still small voice extolling the cardinal virtues or murmuring, on behalf of his own Better Self, 'I am filled with love and compassion for all, so help me God.'

After reading about the Woodland Road Camp, I turned to the second chapter of *Brave New World*. In that chapter the Director of Hatcheries and Conditioning for Western Europe explains to a group of freshman conditioners and hatchers the workings of that state-controlled system of ethical education, known in the seventh century after Ford as Hypnopaedia. The earliest attempts at sleep-teaching, the Director told his

audience, had been misguided, and therefore
unsuccessful. Educators had tried to give intellectual training to their slumbering pupils. But
intellectual activity is incompatible with sleep.
Hypnopaedia became successful only when it was
used for *moral* training – in other words, for the
conditioning of behaviour through verbal suggestion at a time of lowered psychological resistance.
'Wordless conditioning is crude and wholesale,
cannot inculcate the more complex courses of
behaviour required by the State. For that there
must be words, but words without reason' . . . the
kind of words that require no analysis for their
comprehension, but can be swallowed whole by
the sleeping brain. This is true hypnopaedia, 'the
greatest moralizing and socializing force of all
time'. In the *Brave New World*, no citizens belonging to the lower castes ever gave any trouble.
Why? Because, from the moment he could speak
and understand what was said to him, every
lower-caste child was exposed to endlessly repeated suggestions, night after night, during the
hours of drowsiness and sleep. These suggestions
were 'like drops of liquid sealing wax, drops that
adhere, incrust, incorporate themselves with what
they fall on, till finally the rock is all one scarlet
blob. Till at last the child's mind *is* these suggestions and the sum of these suggestions *is* the
child's mind. And not the child's mind only. The
adult's mind too – all his life long. The mind that

judges and desires and decides – made up of these suggestions. But these suggestions are *our* suggestions – suggestions from the State . . .'

To date, so far as I know, hypnopaedic suggestions have been given by no State more formidable than Tulare County, and the nature of Tulare's hypnopaedic suggestions to lawbreakers is unexceptionable. If only all of us, and not only the inmates of the Woodland Road Camp, could be effectively filled, during our sleep, with love and compassion for all! No, it is not the message conveyed by the inspirational whisper that one objects to; it is the principle of sleep-teaching by governmental agencies. Is hypnopaedia the sort of instrument that officials, delegated to exercise authority in a democratic society, ought to be allowed to use at their discretion? In the present instance they are using it only on volunteers and with the best intentions. But there is no guarantee that in other cases the intentions will be good or the indoctrination on a voluntary basis. Any law or social arrangement which makes it possible for officials to be led into temptation is bad. Any law or arrangement which preserves them from being tempted to abuse their delegated power for their own advantage, or for the benefit of the State or of some political, economic or ecclesiastical organization, is good. Hypnopaedia, if it is effective, would be a tremendously powerful instrument in the hands of anyone in a position to impose suggestions upon a captive audience. A democratic society is a society dedicated to the proposition that power is often abused and should therefore be entrusted to officials only in limited amounts and for limited periods of time. In such a society, the use of hypnopaedia by officials should be regulated by law – that is, of course, if hypnopaedia is genuinely an instrument of power. But is it in fact an instrument of power? Will it work now as well as I imagined it working in the seventh century A.F.? Let us examine the evidence.

In the *Psychological Bulletin* for July 1955, Charles W. Simon and William H. Emmons have analysed and evaluated the ten most important studies in the field. All these studies were concerned with memory. Does sleep-teaching help the pupil in his task of learning by rote? And to what extent is material whispered into the ear of a sleeping person remembered next morning when he wakes? Simon and Emmons answer as follows: 'Ten sleep-learning studies were reviewed. Many of these have been cited uncritically by commercial firms or in popular magazines and news articles as evidence in support of the feasibility of learning during sleep. A critical analysis was made of their experimental design, statistics, methodology and criteria of sleep. All the studies had weaknesses in one or more of these areas.' The studies do not make it unequivocally clear that learning during *sleep* actually takes place. But some learning appears to take place in 'a special kind of waking state wherein the subjects do not remember later on if they had been awake. This may be of great practical importance from the standpoint of economy in study time, but it cannot be construed as *sleep learning* ... The problem is partially confounded by an inadequate definition of sleep.'

Meanwhile the fact remains that in the American Army during the Second World War (and even, experimentally, during the First) day-time instruction in the Morse Code and in foreign languages was supplemented by instruction during sleep – apparently with satisfactory results. Since the end of the Second World War several commercial firms in the United States and elsewhere have sold large numbers of pillow speakers and clock-controlled phonographs and tape recorders for the use of actors in a hurry to learn their parts, of politicians and preachers who want to give the illusion of being extemporaneously eloquent, of students preparing for examinations and, finally and most profitably, of the countless people who are dissatisfied with themselves as they are and would like to be suggested or auto-suggested into becoming something else. Self-administered suggestion can easily be recorded on magnetic tape and listened to, over and over again, by day and during sleep.

Suggestions from the outside may be bought in
the form of records carrying a wide variety of
helpful messages. There are on the market records for the release of tension and the induction
of deep relaxation, records for promoting self-
confidence (much used by salesmen), records for
increasing one's charm and making one's personality more magnetic. Among the best sellers are
records for the achievement of sexual harmony
and records for those who wish to lose weight. ('I
am cold to chocolate, insensible to the lure of
potatoes, utterly unmoved by muffins.') There are
records for improved health and even records for
making more money. And the remarkable thing is
that, according to the unsolicited testimonials
sent in by grateful purchasers of these records,
many people actually do make more money after
listening to hypnopaedic suggestions to that effect, many obese ladies do lose weight and many
couples on the verge of divorce achieve sexual
harmony and live happily ever after.

In this context an article by Theordore X.
Barber, 'Sleep and Hypnosis' which appeared in
The Journal of Clinical and Experimental Hypnosis for
October 1956 is most enlightening. Mr Barber
points out that there is a significant difference
between light sleep and deep sleep. In deep sleep
the electro-encephalograph records no alpha
waves; in light sleep alpha waves make their
appearance. In this respect light sleep is closer to

the waking and hypnotic states (in both of which alpha waves are present) than it is to deep sleep. A loud noise will cause a person in deep sleep to awaken. A less violent stimulus will not arouse him, but will cause the reappearance of alpha waves. Deep sleep has given place for the time being to light sleep.

A person in deep sleep is unsuggestible. But when subjects in light sleep are given suggestions, they will respond to them, Mr Barber found, in the same way that they respond to suggestions when in the hypnotic trance.

Many of the earlier investigators of hypnotism made similar experiments. In his classical *History, Practice and Theory of Hypnotism,* first published in 1903, Milne Bramwell records that 'many authorities claim to have changed natural sleep into hypnotic sleep. According to Wetterstrand, it is often very easy to put oneself *en rapport* with sleeping persons, especially children . . . Wetterstrand thinks this method of inducing hypnosis of much practical value and claims to have often used it successfully.' Bramwell cites many other experienced hypnotists (including such eminent authorities as Bernheim, Moll and Forel) to the same effect. Today an experimenter would not speak of 'changing natural into hypnotic sleep'. All he is prepared to say is that light sleep (as opposed to deep sleep without alpha waves) is a state in which many subjects will accept suggestions as readily as they do when under hypnosis. For example, after being told, when lightly asleep, that they will wake up in a little while, feeling extremely thirsty, many subjects will duly wake up with a dry throat and a craving for water. The cortex may be too inactive to think straight; but it is alert enough to respond to suggestions and to pass them on to the autonomic nervous system.

As we have already seen, the well-known Swedish physician and experimenter, Wetterstrand, was especially successful in the hypnotic treatment of sleeping children. In our own day Wetterstrand's methods are followed by a number of pediatricians, who instruct young mothers in the art of giving helpful suggestions to their children during the hours of light sleep. By this kind of hypnopaedia children can be cured of bed wetting and nail biting, can be prepared to go into surgery without apprehension, can be given confidence and reassurance when, for any reason, the circumstances of their life have become distressing. I myself have seen remarkable results achieved by the therapeutic sleep-teaching of small children. Comparable results could probably be achieved with many adults.

For a would-be dictator, the moral of all this is plain. Under proper conditions, hypnopaedia actually works – works, it would seem, about as well as hypnosis. Most of the things that can be done with and to a person in hypnotic trance can be done with and to a person in light sleep. Verbal suggestions can be passed through the somnolent cortex to the mid-brain, the brain stem and the autonomic nervous system. If these suggestions are well conceived and frequently repeated, the bodily functions of the sleeper can be improved or interfered with, new patterns of feeling can be installed and old ones modified, post-hypnotic commands can be given, slogans, formulas and trigger words deeply ingrained in the memory. Children are better hypnopaedic subjects than adults, and the would-be dictator will take full advantage of the fact. Children of nursery-school and kindergarten age will be treated to hypnopaedic suggestions during their afternoon nap. For older children and particularly the children of party members – the boys and girls who will grow up to be leaders, administrators and teachers – there will be boarding schools, in which an excellent day-time education will be supplemented by nightly sleep-teaching. In the case of adults, special attention will be paid to the sick. As Pavlov demonstrated many years ago, strong- minded and resistant dogs become completely suggestible after an operation or when suffering from some debilitating illness. Our dictator will therefore see that every hospital ward is wired for sound. An appendectomy, an accouchement, a bout of pneumonia or hepatitis, can be made the occasion for an intensive course in loyalty and the true faith, a refresher in the principles of the local ideology. Other captive audiences can be found in prisons, in labour camps, in military barracks, on ships at sea, on trains and aeroplanes in the night, in the dismal waiting rooms of bus terminals and railway stations. Even if the hypnopaedic suggestions given to these captive audiences were no more than ten per cent effective, the results would still be impressive and, for a dictator, highly desirable.

From the heightened suggestibility associated with light sleep and hypnosis let us pass to the normal suggestibility of those who are awake – or at least who think they are awake. (In fact, as the Buddhists insist, most of us are half asleep all the time and go through life as somnambulists obeying somebody else's suggestions. Enlightenment is total awakeness. The word 'Buddha' can be translated as 'The Wake'.)

Genetically, every human being is unique and in many ways unlike every other human being. The range of individual variation from the statistical norm is amazingly wide. And the statistical norm, let us remember, is useful only in actuarial calculations, not in real life. In real life there is no such person as the average man. There are only particular men, women and children, each with his or her inborn idiosyncrasies of mind and body, and all trying (or being compelled) to squeeze their biological diversities into the uniformity of some cultural mould.

Suggestibility is one of the qualities that vary significantly from individual to individual. Environmental factors certainly play their part in making one person more responsive to suggestion than another; but there are also, no less certainly, constitutional differences in the suggestibility of individuals. Extreme resistance to suggestion is rather rare. Fortunately so. For if everyone were as unsuggestible as some people are, social life would be impossible. Societies can function with a reasonable degree of efficiency because, in varying degrees, most people are fairly suggestible. Extreme suggestibility is probably about as rare as extreme unsuggestibility. And this also is fortunate. For if most people were as responsive to outside suggestions as the men and women at the extreme limits of suggestibility, free, rational choice would become for the majority of the electorate virtually impossible, and democratic institutions could not survive, or even come into existence.

A few years ago, at the Massachusetts General Hospital, a group of researchers carried out a most illuminating experiment on the pain-relieving effects of placebos. (A placebo is anything which the patient believes to be an active drug, but which in fact is pharmacologically inactive.) In this experiment the subjects were one hundred and sixty-two patients who had just come out of surgery and were all in considerable pain.

Whenever a patient asked for medication to relieve pain, he or she was given an injection, either of morphine or of distilled water. All the patients received some injections of morphine and some of the placebo. About thirty per cent of the patients never obtained relief from the placebo. On the other hand, fourteen per cent obtained relief after *every* injection of distilled water. The remaining fifty-five per cent of the group were relieved by the placebo on some occasions, but not on others.

In what respects did the suggestible reactors differ from the unsuggestible non-reactors? Careful study and testing revealed that neither age nor sex was a significant factor. Men reacted to placebo as frequently as did women, and young people as often as old ones. Nor did intelligence, as measured by the standard tests, seem to be important. The average IQ of the two groups was about the same. It was above all in temperament, in the way they felt about themselves and other people that the members of the two groups were significantly different. The reactors were more co-operative than the non-reactors, less critical and suspicious. They gave the nurses no trouble and thought that the care they were receiving in the hospital was simply 'wonderful'. But though less unfriendly towards others than the non-reactors, the reactors were generally much more anxious about themselves. Under stress, this anxiety tended to translate itself into various

psychosomatic symptoms, such as stomach up-
sets, diarrhea and headaches. In spite of or
because of their anxiety, most of the reactors were
more uninhibited in the display of emotion than
were the non-reactors, and more voluble. They
were also much more religious, much more active
in the affairs of their church and much more
preoccupied, on a subconscious level, with their
pelvic and abdominal organs.

It is interesting to compare these figures for
reaction to placebos with the estimates made, in
their own special field, by writers on hypnosis.
About a fifth of the population, they tell us, can be
hypnotized very easily. Another fifth cannot be
hypnotized at all, or can be hypnotized only when
drugs or fatigue have lowered psychological resistance. The remaining three-fifths can be hypnotized somewhat less easily than the first group,
but considerably more easily than the second. A
manufacturer of hypnopaedic records has told me
that about twenty per cent of his customers are
enthusiastic and report striking results in a very
short time. At the other end of the spectrum of
suggestibility there is an eight per cent minority
that regularly asks for its money back. Between
these two extremes are the people who fail to get
quick results, but are suggestible enough to be
affected in the long run. If they listen persever-
ingly to the appropriate hypnopaedic instructions
they will end by getting what they want – self-

confidence or sexual harmony, less weight or more money.

The ideals of democracy and freedom confront the brute fact of human suggestibility. One-fifth of every electorate can be hypnotized almost in the twinkling of an eye, one-seventh can be relieved of pain by injections of water, one-quarter will respond promptly and enthusiastically to hypnopaedia. And to these all too co- operative minorities must be added the slow- starting majorities, whose less extreme suggestibility can be effectually exploited by anyone who knows his business and is prepared to take the necessary time and trouble.

Is individual freedom compatible with a high degree of individual suggestibility? Can democratic institutions survive the subversion from within of skilled mind- manipulators trained in the science and art of exploiting the suggestibility both of individuals and of crowds? To what extent can the inborn tendency to be too suggestible for one's own good or the good of a democratic society be neutralized by education? How far can the exploitation of inordinate suggestibility by businessmen and ecclesiastics, by politicians in and out of power, be controlled by law? Explicitly or implicitly, the first two questions have been discussed in earlier chapters. In what follows I shall consider the problems of prevention and cure.

XI

Education for Freedom

Education for freedom must begin by stating facts and enunciating values, and must go on to develop appropriate techniques for realizing the values and for combating those who, for whatever reason, choose to ignore the facts or deny the values.

In an earlier chapter I have discussed the Social Ethic, in terms of which the evil resulting from over-organization and overpopulation are justified and made to seem good. Is such a system of values consonant with what we know about human physique and temperament? The Social Ethic assumes that nurture is all-important in determining human behaviour and that nature – the psycho-physical equipment with which individuals are born – is a negligible factor. But is this true? Is it true that human beings are nothing but the products of their social environment? And if it is not true, what justification can there be for maintaining that the individual is less important than the group of which he is a member?

All the available evidence points to the conclusion that in the life of individuals and societies heredity is no less significant than culture. Every individual is biologically unique and unlike all other individuals. Freedom is therefore a great good, tolerance a great virtue and regimentation a great misfortune. For practical or theoretical reasons, dictators, Organization Men and certain scientists are anxious to reduce the maddening diversity of men's natures to some kind of manageable uniformity. In the first flush of his Behaviouristic fervour, J. B. Watson roundly declared that he could find 'no support for hereditary patterns of behaviour, nor for special abilities (musical, art, etc.) which are supposed to run in families'. And even today we find a distinguished psychologist, Professor B. F. Skinner of Harvard, insisting that, 'as scientific explanation becomes more and more comprehensive, the contribution which may be claimed by the individual himself appears to approach zero. Man's vaunted creative powers, his achievements in art, science and morals, his capacity to choose and our right to hold him responsible for the consequences of his choice – none of these is conspicuous in the new scientific self-portrait.' In a word, Shakespeare's plays were not written by Shakespeare, nor even by Bacon or the Earl of Oxford; they were written by Elizabethan England.

More than sixty years ago William James wrote an essay on 'Great Men and their Environment', in which he set out to defend the outstanding individual against the assaults of Herbert

Spencer. Spencer had proclaimed that 'Science' (that wonderfully convenient personification of the opinions, at a given date, of Professors X, Y and Z) had completely abolished the Great Man. 'The great man', he had written, 'must be classed with all other phenomena in the society that gave him birth, as a product of its antecedents.' The great man may be (or seem to be) 'the proximate initiator of changes ... But if there is to be anything like a real explanation of these changes, it must be sought in that aggregate of conditions out of which both he and they have arisen.' This is one of those empty profundities to which no operational meaning can possibly be attached. What our philosopher is saying is that we must know everything before we can fully understand anything. No doubt. But in fact we shall never know everything. We must therefore be content with partial understanding and proximate causes – including the influence of great men. 'If anything is humanly certain', writes William James, 'it is that the great man's society, properly so called, does not make him before he can remake it. Physiological forces with which the social, political, geographical and to a great extent anthropological conditions have just as much and just as little to do as the crater of Vesuvius has to do with the flickering of this gas by which I write, are what make him. Can it be that Mr Spencer holds the convergence of sociological pressures to have so impinged upon Stratford-upon-Avon about the twenty-sixth of April 1564, that a W. Shakespeare, with all his mental peculiarites, had to be born there? ... And does he mean to say that if the aforesaid W. Shakespeare had died of cholera infantium, another mother at Stratford-upon-Avon would needs have engendered a duplicate copy of him, to restore the sociological equilibrium.'

Professor Skinner is an experimental psychologist, and his treatise on 'Science and Human Behavior' is solidly based upon facts. But unfortunately the facts belong to so limited a class that when at last he ventures upon a generalization, his conclusions are as sweepingly unrealistic as those of the Victorian theorizer. Inevitably so; for Professor Skinner's indifference to what James calls the 'physiological forces' is almost as complete as Herbert Spencer's. The genetic factors determining human behaviour are dismissed by him in less than a page. There is no reference in his book to the findings of constitutional medicine, nor any hint of that constitutional psychology, in terms of which (and in terms of which alone, so far as I can judge) it might be possible to write a complete and realistic biography of an individual in relation to the relevant facts of his existence – his body, his temperament, his intellectual endowments, his immediate environment from moment to moment, his time, place and culture. A science of human behaviour is like a science of motion in the abstract – necessary, but, by itself, wholly inadequate to the facts. Consider a dragonfly, a rocket and a breaking wave. All three of them illustrate the same fundamental laws of motion; but they illustrate these laws in different ways, and the differences are at least as important as the identities. By itself, a study of motion can tell us almost nothing about that which, in any given instance, is being moved. Similarly a study of behaviour can, by itself, tell us almost nothing about the individual mind-body that, in any particular instance, is exhibiting the behaviour. But to us who are mind-bodies, a knowledge of mind-bodies is of paramount importance. Moreover, we know by observation and experience that the differences between individual mind-bodies can and do profoundly affect their social environment. On this last point Mr Bertrand Russell is in full agreement with William James – and with practically everyone, I would add, except the proponents of Spencerian or Behaviouristic scientism. In Russell's view the causes of historical change are of three kinds – economic change, political theory and important individuals. 'I do not believe', says Mr Russell, 'that any of these can be ignored, or wholly explained away as the effect of causes of another kind.' Thus, if Bismarck and Lenin had died in infancy, our world would be very different from what, thanks in part to Bismarck and Lenin, it now is. 'History is not yet a science, and can only be made to seem scientific by falsifications and omissions. In real life, life as it is lived from day to day, the individual can never be explained away. It is only in theory that his contributions appear to approach zero; in practice they are all-important. When a piece of work gets done in the world, who actually does it? Whose eyes and ears do the perceiving, whose cortex does the thinking, who has the feelings that motivate, the will that overcomes obstacles? Certainly not the social environment; for a group is not an organism, but only a blind unconscious organization. Everything that is done within a society is done by individuals. These individuals are, of course, profoundly influenced by the local culture, the taboos and moralities, the information and misinformation handed down from the past and preserved in a body of spoken traditions or written literature; but whatever each individual takes from society (or, to be more accurate, whatever he takes from other individuals associated in groups, or from the symbolic records compiled by other individuals, living or dead) will be used by him in his own unique way – with *his* special senses, *his* biochemical make-up, *his* physique and temperament, and nobody else's. No amount of scientific explanation, however comprehensive, can explain away these self-evident facts. And let us remember that Professor Skinner's scientific portrait of man as the product of the social environment is not the only scientific portrait. There are other, more realistic likenesses. Consider, for example, Professor Roger Williams' portrait. What he paints is not behaviour in the abstract, but mind-bodies behaving – mind-bodies that are the products partly of the environment they share with other mind-bodies, partly of their own private heredity. In *The Human Frontier* and *Free but Unequal* Professor Williams has expatiated, with a wealth of detailed evidence, on those innate differences between individuals for which Dr Watson could find no support and whose importance, in Professor Skinner's eyes, approaches zero. Among animals, biological variability within a given species becomes more and more conspicuous as we move up the evolutionary scale. This biological variability is highest in man, and human beings display a greater degree of biochemical, structural and temperamental diversity than do the members of any other species. This is a plain observable fact. But what I have called the Will to Order, the desire to impose a comprehensible uniformity upon the bewildering manifoldness of things and events, has led many people to ignore this fact. They have minimized biological uniqueness and have concentrated all their attention upon the simpler and, in the present state of knowledge, more understandable environmental factors involved in human behaviour. 'As a result of this environmentally centered thinking and investigation,' writes Professor Williams, 'the doctrine of the essential uniformity of human infants has been widely accepted and is held by a great body of social psychologists, sociologists, social anthropologists, and many others, including historians, economists, educationalists, legal scholars and men in public life. This doctrine has been incorporated into the prevailing mode of thought of many who have had to do with shaping educational and governmental policies and is often accepted unquestioningly by those who do little critical thinking of their own.'

An ethical system that is based upon a fairly realistic appraisal of the data of experience is likely to do more good than harm. But many ethical systems have been based upon an appraisal of experience, a view of the nature of things, that is hopelessly unrealistic. Such an ethic is likely to do more harm than good. Thus, until quite recent times, it was universally believed that bad weather, diseases of cattle and sexual impotence could be, and in many cases actually were, caused by the malevolent operations of magicians. To catch and kill magicians was therefore a duty – and this duty, moreover, had been divinely ordained in the second Book of Moses: 'Thou shalt not suffer a witch to live.' The systems of ethics and law that were based upon this erroneous view of the nature of things were the cause (during the centuries when they were taken most seriously by men in authority) of the most appalling evils. The orgy of spying, lynching and judicial murder, which these wrong views about magic made logical and mandatory, was not matched until our own days, when the Communist ethic, based upon erroneous views about race, commanded and justified atrocities on an even greater scale. Consequences hardly less undesirable are likely to follow the general adoption of a Social Ethic, based upon the erroneous view that ours is a fully social species, that human infants are born uniform and that individuals are the product of conditioning by and within the collective environment. If these views were correct, if human beings were in fact the members of a truly social species, and if their individual differences were trifling and could be completely ironed out by appropriate conditioning, then, obviously, there would be no need for liberty and the State would be justified in persecuting the heretics who demanded it. For the individual termite, service to the termitary is perfect freedom. But human beings are not completely social; they are only moderately gregarious. Their societies are not organisms, like the hive or the anthill; they are organizations, in other words *ad hoc* machines for collective living. Moreover, the differences between individuals are so great that, in spite of the most intensive cultural ironing, an extreme endomorph (to use W. H. Sheldon's terminology) will retain his sociable viscerotonic characteristics, an extreme mesomorph will remain energetically somatotonic through thick and thin, and an extreme ectomorph will always be cerebrotonic, introverted and over-sensitive. In the Brave New World of my fable socially desirable behaviour was ensured by a double process of genetic manipulation and post-natal conditioning. Babies were cultivated in bottles and a high de- gree of uniformity in the human product was as- sured by using ova from a limited number of mothers and by treating each ovum in such a way that it would split and split again, producing identical twins in batches of a hundred or more. In this way it was possible to produce standardized machine-minders for standardized machines. And the standardization of the machine-minders was perfected, after birth, by infant conditioning, hypnopaedia and chemically induced euphoria as a substitute for the satisfaction of feeling oneself free and creative. In the world we live in, as has been pointed out in earlier chapters, vast impersonal forces are making for the centralization of power and a regimented society. The genetic standard- ization of individuals is still impossible; but Big Government and Big Business already possess, or will very soon possess, all the techniques for mind-manipulation described in *Brave New World,* along with others of which I was too unimaginative to dream. Lacking the ability to impose genetic uniformity upon embryos, the rulers of tomorrow's overpopulated and over-organized world will try to impose sociál and cultural uniformity upon adults and their children. To achieve this end, they will (unless prevented) make use of all the mind-manipulation techniques at their disposal and will not hesitate to reinforce these methods of non-rational persuasion by economic coercion and threats of physical violence. If this kind of tyranny is to be avoided, we must begin without delay to educate ourselves and our children for freedom and self-government.

Such an education for freedom should be, as I have said, an education first of all in facts and in values – the facts of individual diversity and genetic uniqueness and the values of freedom, tolerance and mutual charity which are the ethical corollaries of these facts. But unfortunately correct knowledge and sound principles are not enough. An unexciting truth may be eclipsed by a thrilling falsehood. A skilful appeal to passion is often too strong for the best of good resolutions. The effects of false and pernicious propaganda cannot be neutralized except by a thorough training in the art of analysing its techniques and seeing through its sophistries. Language has made possible man's progress from animality to civilization. But language has also inspired that sustained folly and that systematic, that genuinely diabolic wickedness which are no less characteristic of human behaviour than are the language-inspired virtues of systematic forethought and sustained angelic benevolence. Language permits its users to pay attention to things, persons and events, even when the things and persons are absent and the events are not taking place. Language gives definition to our memories and, by translating experiences into symbols, converts the immediacy of craving or abhorrence, of hatred or love, into fixed principles of feeling and conduct. In some way of which we are wholly unconscious, the reticular system of the brain selects from a countless host of stimuli those few experiences which are of practical importance to us. From these unconsciously selected experiences we more or less consciously select and abstract a smaller number, which we label with words from our vocabulary and then classify within a system at once metaphysical, scientific and ethical, made up of other words on a higher level of abstraction. In cases where the selecting and abstracting have been dictated by a system that is not too erroneous as a view of the nature of things, and where the verbal labels have been intelligently chosen and their symbolic nature clearly understood, our behaviour is apt to be realistic and tolerably decent. But under the influence of badly chosen words, applied, without any understanding of their merely symbolic character, to experiences that have been selected and abstracted in the light of a system of erroneous ideas, we are apt to behave with a fiendishness and an organized stupidity, of which dumb animals (precisely because they *are* dumb and cannot speak) are blessedly incapable.

In their anti-rational propaganda the enemies of freedom systematically pervert the resources of language in order to wheedle or stampede their victims into thinking, feeling and acting as they, the mind-manipulators, want them to think, feel and act. An education for freedom (and for the love and intelligence which are at once the conditions and the results of freedom) must be, among other things, an education in the proper uses of language. For the last two or three generations philosophers have devoted a great deal of time and thought to the analysis of symbols and the meaning of meaning. How are the words and sentences which we speak related to the things, persons and events, with which we have to deal in our day-to-day living? To discuss this problem would take too long and lead us too far afield. Suffice it to say that all the intellectual materials for a sound education in the proper use of language – an education on every level from the kindergarten to the post-graduate school – are now available. Such an education in the art of disting-

uishing between the proper and the improper use
of symbols could be inaugurated immediately.
Indeed it might have been inaugurated at any
time during the last thirty or forty years. And yet
children are nowhere taught, in any systematic
way, to distinguish true from false, or meaningful
from meaningless, statements. Why is this so?
Because their elders, even in the democratic
countries, do not want them to be given this kind
of education. In this context the brief, sad history
of the Institute for Propaganda Analysis is highly
significant. The Institute was founded in 1937,
when Nazi propaganda was at its noisiest and
most effective, by Mr Filene, the New England
philanthropist. Under its auspices analyses of
non-rational propaganda were made and several
texts for the instruction of high school and
university students were prepared. Then came
the war – a total war on all the fronts, the mental
no less than the physical. With all the Allied
Governments engaging in 'Psychological War-
fare' an insistence upon the desirability of analysing propaganda seemed a bit tactless. The Institute was closed in 1941. But even before the
outbreak of hostilities, there were many persons
to whom its activities seemed profoundly objectionable. Certain educators, for example, disap-
proved of the teaching of propaganda analysis on
the grounds that it would make adolescents unduly cynical. Nor was it welcomed by the military

authorities, who were afraid that recruits might
start to analyse the utterances of drill sergeants.
And then there were the clergymen and the
advertisers. The clergymen were against propaganda analysis as tending to undermine belief
and diminish church-going; the advertisers objec-
ted on the grounds that it might undermine brand
loyalty and reduce sales.

These fears and dislikes were not unfounded.
Too searching a scrutiny by too many of the
common folk of what is said by their pastors and
masters might prove to be profoundly subversive.
In its present form, the social order depends for
its continued existence on the acceptance, without
too many embarrassing questions, of the propaganda put forth by those in authority and the
propaganda hallowed by the local traditions. The
problem, once more, is to find the happy mean.
Individuals must be suggestible enough to be
willing and able to make their society work, but
not so suggestible as to fall helplessly under the
spell of professional mind-manipulators. Similarly, they should by taught enough about propaganda analysis to preserve them from an uncritical belief in sheer nonsense, but not so much as to
make them reject outright the not always rational
outpourings of the well-meaning guardians of
tradition. Probably the happy mean between
gullibility and a total skepticism can never be
discovered and maintained by analysis alone.

This rather negative approach to the problem will have to be supplemented by something more positive – the enunciation of a set of generally acceptable values based upon a solid foundation of facts. The value, first of all, of individual freedom, based upon the facts of human diversity and genetic uniqueness; the value of charity and compassion, based upon the old familiar fact, lately rediscovered by modern psychiatry – the fact that, whatever their mental and physical diversity, love is as necessary to human beings as food and shelter; and finally the value of intelligence, without which love is impotent and freedom unattainable. This set of values will provide us with a criterion by which propaganda may be judged. The propaganda that is found to be both nonsensical and immoral may be rejected out of hand. That which is merely irrational, but compatible with love and freedom, and not on principle opposed to the exercise of intelligence, may be provisionally accepted for what it is worth.

XII

What can be Done?

We can be educated for freedom — much better educated for it than we are at present. But freedom, as I have tried to show, is threatened from many directions, and these threats are of many different kinds — demographic, social, political, psychological. Our disease has a multiplicity of co-operating causes and is not to be cured except by a multiplicity of co-operating remedies. In coping with any complex human situation, we must take account of all the relevant factors, not merely of a single factor. Nothing short of everything is ever really enough. Freedom is menaced, and education for freedom is urgently needed. But so are many other things — for example, social organization for freedom, birth control for freedom, legislation for freedom. Let us begin with the last of these items.

From the time of Magna Carta and even earlier, the makers of English law have been concerned to protect the physical freedom of the individual. A person who is being kept in prison on grounds of doubtful legality has the right under the Common Law as clarified by the statute of 1679, to appeal to one of the higher courts of justice for a writ of *habeas corpus*. This writ is addressed by a judge of the high court to a sheriff or jailer, and commands him, within a specified period of time, to bring the person he is holding in custody to the court for an examination of his case – to bring, be it noted, not the person's written complaint, nor his legal representatives, but his *corpus*, his body, the too too solid flesh which has been made to sleep on boards, to smell the fetid prison air, to eat the revolting prison food. This concern with the basic condition of freedom – the absence of physical constraint – is unquestionably necessary, but is not all that is necessary. It is perfectly possible for a man to be out of prison, and yet not free – to be under no physical constraint and yet to be a psychological captive, compelled to think, feel and act as the representatives of the national state, or of some private interest within the nation, wants him to think, feel and act. There will never be such a thing as a writ of *habeas mentem*; for no sheriff or jailer can bring an illegally imprisoned mind into court, and no person whose mind had been made captive by the methods outlined in earlier chapters would be in a position to complain of his captivity. The nature of psychological compulsion is such that those who act under constraint remain under the impression that they are acting on their own initiative. The victim of mind-manipulation does not know that he is a victim.

To him, the walls of his prison are invisible, and he believes himself to be free. That he is not free is apparent only to other people. His servitude is strictly objective.

No, I repeat, there can never be such a thing as a writ of *habeas mentem*. But there *can* be preventive legislation – an outlawing of the psychological slave trade, a statute for the protection of minds against the unscrupulous purveyors of poisonous propaganda, modelled on the statutes for the protection of bodies against the unscrupulous purveyors of adulterated food and dangerous drugs. For example, there could and, I think, there should be legislation limiting the right of public officials, civil or military, to subject the captive audiences under their command or in their custody to sleep teaching. There could and, I think, there should be legislation prohibiting the use of subliminal projection in public places or on television screens. There could and, I think, there should be legislation to prevent political candidates not merely from spending more than a certain amount of money on their election campaigns, but also to prevent them from resorting to the kind of anti-rational propaganda that makes nonsense of the whole democratic process.

Such preventive legislation might do some good; but if the great impersonal forces now menacing freedom continue to gather momentum, they cannot do much good for very long.

The best of constitutions and preventive laws will be powerless against the steadily increasing pressures of overpopulation and of the over-organization imposed by growing numbers and advancing technology. The constitutions will not be abrogated and the good laws will remain on the statute book; but these liberal forms will merely serve to mask and adorn a profoundly illiberal substance. Given unchecked overpopulation and over-organization, we may expect to see in the democratic countries a reversal of the process which transformed England into a democracy, while retaining all the outward forms of a monarchy. Under the relentless thrust of accelerating overpopulation and increasing over-organization, and by means of ever more effective methods of mind-manipulation, the democracies will change their nature; the quaint old forms – elections, parliaments, Supreme Courts and all the rest – will remain. The underlying substance will be a new kind of non-violent totalitarianism. All the traditional names, all the hallowed slogans will remain exactly what they were in the good old days. Democracy and freedom will be the theme of every broadcast and editorial – but democracy and freedom in a strictly Pickwickian sense. Meanwhile the ruling oligarchy and its highly trained élite of soldiers, policemen, thought-manufacturers and mind-manipulators will quietly run the show as they see fit.

How can we control the vast impersonal forces that now menace our hard-won freedoms? On the verbal level and in general terms, the question may be answered with the utmost ease. Consider the problem of overpopulation. Rapidly mounting human numbers are pressing ever more heavily on natural resources. What is to be done? Obviously we must, with all possible speed, reduce the birth rate to the point where it does not exceed the death rate. At the same time we must, with all possible speed, increase food production, we must institute and implement a world-wide policy for conserving our soils and our forests, we must develop practical substitutes, preferably less dangerous and less rapidly exhaustible than uranium, for our present fuels; and, while husbanding our dwindling resources of easily available minerals, we must work out new and not too costly methods for extracting these minerals from ever poorer and poorer ores – the poorest ore of all being sea water. But all this, needless to say, is almost infinitely easier said than done. The annual increase of numbers should be reduced. But how? We are given two choices – famine, pestilence and war on the one hand, birth control on the other. Most of us choose birth control – and immediately find ourselves confronted by a problem that is simultaneously a puzzle in physiology, pharmacology, sociology, psychology and even theology. 'The Pill' has not yet been perfected.

When and if it is perfected, how can it be
distributed to the many hundreds of millions of
potential mothers (or, if it is a pill that works
upon the male, potential fathers) who will have to
take it if the birth-rate of the species is to be
reduced? And, given existing social customs and
the forces of cultural and psychological inertia,
how can those who ought to take the pill, but
don't want to, be persuaded to change their
minds? And what about the objections on the part
of the Roman Catholic Church to any form of
birth control except the so-called Rhythm
Method – a method incidentally, which has
proved, hitherto, to be almost completely ineffec-
tive in reducing the birth-rate of those industrially
backward societies where such a reduction is most
urgently necessary? And these questions about
the hypothetically perfect Pill must be asked, with
as little prospect of eliciting satisfactory answers,
about the chemical and mechanical methods of
birth control already available.

When we pass from the problems of birth
control to the problems of increasing the available
food supply and conserving our natural resources,
we find ourselves confronted by difficulties not
perhaps quite so great, but still enormous. There
is the problem, first of all, of education. How soon
can the innumerable peasants and farmers, who
are now responsible for raising most of the world's
supply of food, be educated into improving their

methods? And when and if they are educated,
where will they find the capital to provide them
with the machines, the fuel and lubricants, the
electric power, the fertilizers and the improved
strains of food-plants and domestic animals, without which the best agricultural education is use-
less? Similarly, who is going to educate the
human race in the principles and practice of
conservation? And how are the hungry peasant-
citizens of a country whose population and demands for food are rapidly rising, be prevented
from 'mining the soil'? And, if they can be
prevented, who will pay for their support while
the wounded and exhausted earth is being gra-
dually nursed back, if that is still feasible, to
health and restored fertility? Or consider the
backward societies that are now trying to indust-
rialize. If they succeed, who is to prevent them, in
their desperate effort to catch up and keep up,
from squandering the planet's irreplaceable resources as stupidly and wantonly as was done,
and is still being done, by their forerunners in the
race? And when the day of reckoning comes,
where, in the poorer countries, will anyone find
the scientific manpower and the huge amounts of
capital that will be required to extract the indispensable minerals from ores in which their concentration is too low, under existing circumstances, to make extraction technically feasible or
economically justifiable? It may be that, in time, a

practical answer to all these questions can be found. But in how much time? In any race between human numbers and natural resources, time is against us. By the end of the present century, there may, if we try very hard, be twice as much food on the world's markets as there is today. But there will also be about twice as many people, and several billions of these people will be living in partially industrialized countries and consuming ten times as much power, water, timber and irreplaceable minerals as their parents are consuming now. In a word, the food situation will be as bad as it is today, and the raw materials situation will be considerably worse.

To find a solution to the problem of over-organization is hardly less difficult than to find a solution to the problem of natural resources and increasing numbers. On the verbal level and in general terms, the answer is perfectly simple. Thus, it is a political axiom that power follows property. But it is now a historical fact that the means of production are fast becoming the monopolistic property of Big Business and Big Government. Therefore, if you believe in democracy, make arrangements to distribute property as widely as possible.

Or take the right to vote. In principle, it is a great privilege. In practice, as recent history has repeatedly shown, the right to vote, by itself, is no guarantee of liberty. Therefore, if you wish to avoid dictatorship by plebiscite, break up modern society's vast, machine-like collectives into self-governing, voluntarily co-operating groups, capable of functioning outside the bureaucratic systems of Big Business and Big Government.

Overpopulation and over-organization have produced the modern metropolis, in which a fully human life of multiple personal relationships has become almost impossible. Therefore, if you wish to avoid the spiritual impoverishment of individuals and whole societies, leave the metropolis and revive the small country community, or alternatively humanize the metropolis by creating within its network of mechanical organizations the urban equivalents of small country communities, in which individuals can meet and co-operate as complete persons, not as the mere embodiments of specialized functions.

All this is obvious today and, indeed, was obvious fifty years ago. From Hilaire Belloc to Mr Mortimer Adler, from the early apostles of co-operative credit unions to the land reformers of modern Italy and Japan, men of good will have for generations been advocating the decentralization of economic power and the wide-spread distribution of property. And how many ingenious schemes have been propounded for the dispersal of production, for a return to small scale 'village industry'. And then there were Dubreuil's elaborate plans for giving a measure of autonomy and initiative to the various departments of a single large industrial organization. There were the Syndicalists, with their blueprints for a stateless society organized as a federation of productive groups under the auspices of the trade unions. In America Arthur Morgan and Baker Brownell have set forth the theory and described the practice of a new kind of community living on the village and small town level.

Professor Skinner of Harvard has set forth a psychologist's view of the problem in his *Walden Two,* a Utopian novel about a self-sustaining and autonomous community so scientifically organized that nobody is ever led into anti-social temptation and, without resort to coercion or undesirable propaganda, everyone does what he or she ought to do, and everyone is happy and creative. In France, during and after the Second World War, Marcel Barbu and his followers set up a number of self-governing, non-hierarchical communities of production, which were also communities for mutual aid and fully human living. And meanwhile, in London, the Peckham Experiment has demonstrated that it is possible, by coordinating health services with the wider interests of the group, to create a true community even in a metropolis.

We see, then, that the disease of over-organization has been clearly recognized, that various comprehensive remedies have been prescribed and that experimental treatments of symptoms have been attempted here and there, often with considerable success. And yet, in spite of all this preaching and this exemplary practice, the disease grows steadily worse. We know that it is unsafe to allow power to be concentrated in the hands of a ruling oligarchy; nevertheless power is in fact being concentrated in fewer and fewer hands. We know that, for most people, life in a huge modern city is anonymous, atomic, less than fully human; nevertheless the huge cities grow steadily huger and the pattern of urban-industrial living remains unchanged. We know that, in a very large complex society, democracy is almost meaningless except in relation to autonomous groups of manageable size; nevertheless more and more of every nation's affairs are managed by the bureaucrats of Big Government and Big Business. It is only too evident that, in practice, the problem of over-organization is almost as hard to solve as the problem of overpopulation. In both cases we know what ought to be done; but in neither case have we been able, as yet, to act effectively upon our knowledge.

At this point we find ourselves confronted by a very disquieting question: Do we really wish to act upon our knowledge? Does a majority of the population think it worth while to take a good deal of trouble, in order to halt and, if possible, reverse the current drift towards totalitarian control of everything? In the United States – and America is the prophetic image of the rest of the urban-industrial world as it will be a few years from now – recent public opinion polls have revealed that an actual majority of young people in their teens, the voters of tomorrow, have no faith in democratic institutions, see no objection to the censorship of unpopular ideas, do not believe that government of the people by the people is possible, and would be perfectly content, if they can continue to live in the style to which the boom has accustomed them, to be ruled, from above, by an oligarchy of assorted experts. That so many of the well-fed young television-watchers in the world's most powerful democracy should be so completely indifferent to the idea of self-government, so blankly uninterested in freedom of thought and the right to dissent, is distressing, but not too surprising. 'Free as a bird', we say, and envy the winged creatures for their power of unrestricted movement in all the three dimensions. But, alas, we forget the dodo. Any bird that has learned how to grub up a good living without being compelled to use its wings will soon renounce the privilege of flight and remain forever grounded. Something analogous is true of human beings. If the bread is supplied regularly and copiously three times a day, many of them will be perfectly content to live by bread alone – or at least by bread and circuses alone. 'In the end', says the Grand Inquisitor in

Dostoevsky's parable, 'in the end they will lay their freedom at our feet and say to us, "Make us your slaves, but feed us."' And when Alyosha Karamazov asks his brother, the teller of the story, if the Grand Inquisitor is speaking ironically, Ivan answers: 'Not a bit of it! He claims it as a merit for himself and his Church that they have vanquished freedom and done so to make men happy.' Yes to make men happy: 'for nothing', the Inquisitor insists, 'has ever been more insupportable for a man or a human society than freedom.' Nothing, except the absence of freedom; for when things go badly, and the rations are reduced and the slave drivers step up their demands, the grounded dodos will clamour again for their wings – only to renounce them, yet once more, when times grow better and the dodo-farmers become more lenient and generous. The young people who now think so poorly of democracy may grow up to become fighters for freedom. The cry of 'Give me television and hamburgers, but don't bother me with the responsibilities of liberty', may give place, under altered circumstances, to the cry of 'Give me Liberty or give me death'. If such a revolution takes place, it will be due in part to the operation of forces over which even the most powerful rulers have very little control, in part to the incompetence of those rulers, their inability to make effective use of the mind-manipulating instruments with which science and technology have supplied, and will go on supplying, the would-be tyrant. Considering how little they knew and how poorly they were equipped, the Grand Inquisitors of earlier times did remarkably well. But their successors, the well-informed, thoroughly scientific dictators of the future, will undoubtedly be able to do a great deal better. The Grand Inquisitor reproaches Christ with having called upon men to be free and tells Him that 'we have corrected Thy work and founded it upon miracle, mystery and authority'. But miracle, mystery and authority are not enough to guarantee the indefinite survival of a dictatorship. In my fable of *Brave New World*, the dictators had added science to the list and thus were able to enforce their authority by manipulating the bodies of embryos, the reflexes of infants, and the minds of children and adults. And instead of merely talking about miracles and hinting symbolically at mysteries, they were able, by means of drugs, to give their subjects the direct experience of mysteries and miracles – to transform mere faith into ecstatic knowledge. The older dictators fell because they could never supply their subjects with enough bread, enough circuses, enough miracles and mysteries. Nor did they possess a really effective system of mind-manipulation. In the past free-thinkers and revolutionaries were often the products of the most piously orthodox education. This is not surprising. The methods employed by orthodox educators were and still are extremely inefficient. Under a scientific dictator education will really work – with the result that most men and women will grow up to love their servitude and will never dream of revolution. There seems to be no good reason why a thoroughly scientific dictatorship should ever be overthrown.

Meanwhile there is still freedom left in the world. Many young people, it is true, do not seem to value freedom. But some of us still believe that, without freedom, human beings cannot become fully human and that freedom is therefore supremely valuable. Perhaps the forces that now menace freedom are too strong to be resisted for very long. It is still our duty to do whatever we can to resist them.

Aldous Huxley

Brave New World

With an Introduction by David Bradshaw

Far in the future, the World Controller has finally created the ideal society. In laboratories worldwide, genetic science has brought the human race to perfection. From the Alpha-plus mandarin class to the Epsilon Semi-Morons, designed to perform menial tasks, man is bred and educated to be blissfully content with his pre-destined role.

But, in the Central London Hatchery and Conditioning Centre, Bernard Marx is unhappy. Harbouring an unnatural desire for solitude, feeling only distaste for the endless pleasures of compulsory promiscuity, Bernard has an ill-defined longing to break free. A visit to one of the few remaining Savage Reservations where the old, imperfect life still continues, may be the cure for his distress . . .

Extraordinarily prophetic, *Brave New World* is one of the most influential books of our century.

'A brilliant *tour de force*, *Brave New World* may be read as a grave warning of the pitfalls that await uncontrolled scientific advance. Full of barbed wit and malice-spiced frankness, *Brave New World* is one of the most urgent appeals for a reconciliation of science with religion that our age has known.'   *Observer*

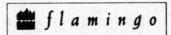 *flamingo*

Aldous Huxley

Antic Hay

With a Foreword by David Lodge

'Few present-day writers would dare to be so heroically encyclo-
paedic, such ardent gleaners of gossip and table-talk as well as of
the profounder reveries of literature, history, science and
religion. Huxley brings an extraordinary vigour and gusto to
every page he writes.'   *Spectator*

When Theodore Gumbril hits upon the notion of designing a type
of pneumatic trouser ('a comfort to all travellers, indispensable to
first-nighters, the concert-goers' friend') to ease the discomfort of
the sedentary life, he decides the time has come to leave his
position as a housemaster in a boys' public school and seek his
fortune in the metropolis.

But post-First-World-War London seems to be gripped by a fever
of hedonism. Gumbril is soon caught up in the delirious world of
aesthetes extraordinaire Mercaptan, Casimir Lypiatt and the
thoroughly civilized Myra Viveash, and finds his burning
ambitions are beginning to lose their urgency . . .

A contemporary commentator coined the word 'futilitarian' to
describe the type of desultory, pleasure-seeking intellectual
Huxley pinned so mercilessly to the literary map in *Antic Hay*.
Wickedly funny and deliciously barbed, the novel epitomises the
glittering neuroticism of its decade.

 *flamingo*

MODERN CLASSIC

Aldous Huxley

Point Counter Point

With an Introduction by David Bradshaw

'Huxley's style is at once dry and rich, intellectual and sensuous, scholarly and romantic. *Point Counter Point* is extremely funny with passages of rich and gorgeous farce.' *Observer*

In Twenties London, the writers, artists, wastrels and dilettantes who frequent Lady Edward Tantamount's Pall Mall parties are permanently engaged in pushing forward the moral frontiers of the age. Marjorie Carling has left her family to live with the writer, Walter Bidlake; the luscious but cold-hearted Lucy Tantamount is set on devouring every man in sight; the repulsive Spandrell insists on entertaining everyone with his accounts of how he debauches young girls; and even Lady Tantamount herself, long tired of her husband and his unwavering devotion to the study of newts, has taken a lover – the fashionable painter and expert taker of virginities, John Bidlake. Only Rampion is left to maintain standards of decency in this increasingly degenerate world . . .

Often described as a *Vanity Fair* for the Twenties. *Point Counter Point* contains wickedly accurate portraits of D. H. Lawrence, Katherine Mansfield, Ottoline Morrell and Huxley himself.

'As a piece of satire, often brilliant, sometimes wise, *Point Counter Point* is a monstrous exposure of a society which confuses pleasure with happiness, sensation with sensibility, mood with opinion, opinion with conviction and self with God.' *Guardian*

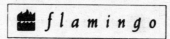

Aldous Huxley

The Doors of Perception
Heaven and Hell

With a Foreword by J. G. Ballard

'Concise, evocative, wise and, above all, humane, *The Doors of Perception* is a masterpiece.'
Sunday Times

One bright May morning in 1953, Aldous Huxley took four-tenths of a gramme of mescalin, sat down and waited to see what would happen. When he opened his eyes, everything, from the flowers in a vase to the creases in his grey flannel trousers, was completely transformed. 'A bunch of flowers shining with their own inner light. Those folds – what a labyrinth of endlessly significant complexity! I was seeing what Adam had seen on the morning of his own creation – the miracle, moment by moment, of naked existence.'

With an astonishing immediacy, Aldous Huxley described his first experience of this new 'sacramental vision of reality' in his famous 1954 essay *The Doors of Perception*. In its 1956 sequel, *Heaven and Hell*, Huxley, reflecting on his earlier mescalin experience, went on to explore the history and nature of mystics and mysticism. Hugely influential, still bristling with a sense of excitement and discovery, these intense and illuminating writings remain the most extraordinary accounts of the visionary experience ever written.

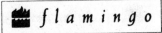 *flamingo*

Aldous Huxley

Crome Yellow

With an Introduction by Malcolm Bradbury

'Delightful. *Crome Yellow* is witty, wordly and poetic.' *The Times*

Denis Stone, a tender young poet, is invited to spend the weekend in the rarefied atmosphere of Crome, renowned for its gatherings of 'bright young things'. Hosted by the world-weary Henry Wimbush and his exotic wife Priscilla, the weekend has much to offer the ingenuous and excitable Denis. From the flaxen-haired Mary Bracegirdle, a student of psychoanalysis, to the ravishing, raven-haired Misses Lapith, the possibilities for romantic intrigue are endless. But just below the witty, glittering surface lurk distinctly sinister and ignoble motives, destined to bring the starry-eyed Denis back to earth with a nasty bump.

First published in 1921, *Crome Yellow* was Aldous Huxley's much-acclaimed debut novel. With the evident relish of the true satirist, he mocked the fads, foibles and spirit of his time with an unsurpassed wit and brilliance. The Twenties have never been better represented – or more entertainingly dismissed.

'With a strong, delightful and admirable talent for caricature, Huxley is at his entertaining best in his grimaces at modern movements and at the ridiculous earnestness of the young.'

Observer

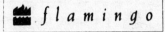 *flamingo*

Aldous Huxley

Eyeless in Gaza

With an Introduction by David Bradshaw

'*Eyeless in Gaza* embodies Huxley's conclusions about life. Amusing, moving and brilliant, there is no doubting the sincerity and the beauty of this book.'
Listener

Anthony Beavis, a *dilettante* social theorist, is a man inclined to recoil from life. The pleasures of the physical world disgust him and the universe of ideas is but a poor refuge. Having long lost the art of intimacy, he betrays friendships and toys cruelly with the affections of women. But as Beavis approaches middle age, his world of perfect detachment begins to lose its appeal. Finally realising that his withdrawal from life has been motivated not by intellectual honesty but by moral cowardice, Beavis, devastated and at crisis point, meets the remarkable and redoubtable Dr Miller . . .

Eyeless in Gaza offers a counterpoint to the biting cynicism of Huxley's earlier satirical novels, and is considered by many to be his definitive work of fiction.

'In *Eyeless in Gaza*, the play of ideas and theories, moral, psychological and sociological, is profuse and scintillating.'
Times Literary Supplement

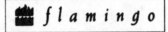

Aldous Huxley

Island

With an Introduction by David Bradshaw

'In the whole history of world literature, no writer has been better equipped to create images of false and true utopias than Aldous Huxley. Even when he has been satirizing the false, the true has always been implicit in his work. We cannot deny *Island*'s brilliance, its learning and its honest attempt to answer the big human questions.'

Anthony Burgess

For over a hundred years the Pacific island of Pala has been the scene of a unique experiment in civilization. At the instigation of a Scottish doctor and a Buddhist king, western science has been brought together with the philosophy and humanism of the East, making the island community a paradise on earth. When Will Farnaby, a cynical, disillusioned journalist, arrives in their midst on an undisclosed search for information about Pala's massive unexploited oil reserves, he is taken wholeheartedly under the islanders' wing. Drawn ever further into their trust, he becomes convinced that this extraordinary way of life should remain unspoilt. Soon, the need to complete his mission becomes an intolerable burden . . .

If *Brave New World* is Huxley's glimpse into hell, then *Island* is his vision of utopia. In this, his last novel, mankind is portrayed at its sanest and most admirable.

'*Island*'s theme is integration and Huxley uses this with disconcerting brilliance. The familiar coruscation of his writing is shown here at its best.'

Guardian

flamingo